PMP®
EXAM PREP

Review Material,
Insider Tips,
Exercises, Games, and
Sample Exams
To Pass
PMI®'s PMP® Exam

ISBN 1-890676-42-X

Printed in the United States of America
02   01   00   99   5   4

For more information visit the RMC – Project management web site:
www.rmcproject.com

Introduction to the Second Edition

It has always been my intention to update this book frequently to make sure that it contains the most current materials available. I am very pleased that the first edition has sold out just months after its initial offering.

This edition takes into account hundreds of comments from my students. I have added new topics that have appeared on the exam, new exercises, and expanded many descriptions. I have also added more difficult questions and fine-tuned many exercises. It should make your study time even more efficient. Most of the people who purchase this book only study about 80 to 100 hours!

NEW CD-ROM – This edition is also designed to work with my new CD test simulation called "PM Warrior" available in the summer of 2000. It contains both a PMBOK® simulation mode and a PMP® Exam simulation that helps you get even more prepared for the exam. The CD contains twice as many questions as the book. In order for people to obtain the CD quickly, I have set up a connection to the distributor through my website, www.rmcproject.com. Check there for the latest details. You do not need the CD to pass the exam, but a substantial number of students have told me that it made a big difference and helped them increase their score.

RAVE REVIEWS FROM AROUND THE WORLD! –
"I have seen all the PMP prep material out there and even attended other classes. Your material is unbelievably far and away the best!"

"I would like to thank you for writing your book - without it I would never have passed the PMP! Your advice on how to approach the exam, the topics that you covered, and the level of questions were spot on. I am based in Cayman so I was studying for the exam purely by myself. Your book helped provide a structured way to approach the exam and covered and provided advice on many topics not in the PMBOK. The examples that require working through difficult topics such as PERT, earned value and working out critical paths enabled me to get full marks in the exam. I think the personal touch that you brought to the book also helped make things so easy to remember. I am recommending your book to a number of people who I have met."

"I just wrote the PMP exam and passed with a good margin. I wanted to drop this note to let you know how valuable I found your PMP Exam Prep book in preparing for the exam. This is without a doubt the most valuable resource I used during my study. Of the two other guides I used, the sample questions you developed most closely emulated those on the actual exam. I found your tips and games very useful in remembering concepts and formulae on the exam. This is a very easy to use book that focuses on the areas critical for study. It simplifies preparation by boiling down the myriad of books suggested as resources to help prepare for the exam. Thanks for putting this excellent resource together."

Table of Contents

An Important Introduction

This book is the result of over seven years experience and feedback from working with more than 2,500 project managers to prepare to take the Project Management Institute's Project Management Professional (PMP®) Exam. So many people have contacted me to say that they appreciated how much the materials helped them to zero in on what they needed to know and gave them "all the tricks they needed to pass." Many even said "I owe it all to you!" So I thought I would share these tricks and materials with you.

I have had access to all the available materials to help pass the PMP® exam. I believe that this book is the most complete, focused, and insightful book available on the exam. There is nothing like this book available from any other source! Other materials are essentially just practice exams or textbooks. I have included practice exams but also exercises, activities, games, pictures, adult learning theory and other tricks to help you prepare for the exam and test yourself along the way. In addition, this book contains hundreds of sample questions *within* the review materials. These features will help you prepare in the shortest possible time, increase your confidence, and tell you what you need to study and what you just need to review. Please contact me to let me know what you think!

Although you will certainly learn a lot about project management, this book is not designed to teach you all you need to know to manage a project, or the art and science of project management. It is designed to:
- Provide a review for the PMP® exam
- Provide insider tips about the exam that are not readily available
- Provide "tricks" for studying and taking the exam
- Shorten your study time
- Help you determine what you know and do not know
- Describe in enough detail the areas most people need to know more about
- Help you determine what to study and focus on
- Tell you what areas are emphasized on the exam
- Help you gain familiarity with the types of questions on the exam
- Increase your probability of passing the exam

Be aware that PMI® has certain experience and education requirements to take the exam (see www.pmi.org for details). The exam serves as a standard for the practice of project management. It contains "standard" practices that I have found many experienced project managers have never heard. As a result, it is difficult to pass the exam without formal training in project management or detailed self-study. If you have not had any formal training in project management or are unfamiliar with the step-by-step process of project management, I suggest my *"Tricks of the Trade for Project Management"* or *"PMP® Exam Prep"* courses.

ARE YOU READY FOR THE EXAM? – I frequently meet people who have been working on projects for many years and therefore believe they know project management. They are very often wrong! I worked on over $1 billion of projects before I learned project management. My students strongly suggest that people who have no formal training in project management tools and techniques delivered by a PMP® take such a class or read other books before they take the exam. You cannot use only your real world experience to take this exam! You will find it exceedingly difficult to answer the "What do you do in this situation?" type questions.

To help you determine if you really know project management before you study for the exam, I have included the following short list as a test. Good luck!

How do you know if you need to improve your knowledge of project management?

PART 1: If you have many of the following problems on projects:
- Cost or schedule overruns
- Unrealistic schedules
- Changing scope of work or schedules
- Poor communication and increased conflict
- Running out of time near the end of the project
- Wasted project efforts
- Unsatisfactory quality
- Low morale
- Projects take too much of your time
- People on the team are unsure of what needs to be done
- Rework
- Too many project meetings

PART 2: If you do not know or do not use at least two of the following:
- Project charter
- Work breakdown structure
- Network diagram
- Critical path
- PERT
- PERT estimating
- Earned value
- Parametric estimating
- Standard deviation
- Managing by exception to the plan
- Risk management
- Expected value
- Calculating budget reserves

USING THIS BOOK
PMBOK® This book is intended to work hand in hand with PMI®'s A Guide to the Project Management Body of Knowledge. For the sake of brevity, this Guide will be referred to in this book as the PMBOK®. All page references in this document are to the PMBOK® unless otherwise stated! You need both the PMBOK® and this book to prepare for the exam. The PMBOK® can be downloaded for free from PMI® at www.pmi.org.

INDIVIDUAL USE – This book is intended for individual use because the person using it will need to and want to write the answers to the exercises. If more than one person uses this book, it will severely undermine the effectiveness of these materials.

THE MATERIALS – Each chapter in the book is organized the same way: an introductory paragraph, a list of "Hot Topics', review material, and a sample exam.

> **INTRODUCTIONS** – The introductory paragraph will give you an overview of the chapter and provide some important overall information.

> **HOT TOPICS** – The "Hot Topics" list will give you an understanding of what topics are important and my impression as to their order of importance. These "Hot Topics" are also listed in bold face in the body of the text as a reminder as you read through the material.

> **REVIEW MATERIALS** – The review materials are current. They are organized by PMBOK® chapter to decrease study time and help students focus. It is more efficient to study one topic and then test yourself on that material. If you answer the questions for a topic correctly, you may not need to study that topic any further. (Please note that the new PMP® exam is no longer given topic by topic.)

> My approach to writing this book is to use lists and summaries whenever appropriate instead of long-winded paragraphs. This cuts down on reading, increases retention and works well for people who want to study fast and effectively. Feedback from students indicates that the review material has missed NONE of the major items on the exam.

> Although PMI® says that answers on the exam will no longer be direct quotations from the PMBOK®, there are many instances where knowing a definition will help you select the correct answer. I have therefore included definitions for memorization.

> **SAMPLE EXAMS** – The sample exams are placed at the end of each chapter so you can review material, test yourself and move on to the next chapter. I suggest that you also take all the sample exams in one sitting to simulate the 4½-hour exam and prepare for the testing environment.

> The sample exam questions are the same length as the real exam, 200 questions. Please note that the body of each chapter also contains exercises and questions. These are also samples of what you can see on the exam.

OTHER MATERIAL – a CD-ROM simulating the PMP® exam with hundreds of additional questions is available starting in the summer of 2000. It is our objective to provide you with the best possible product but not to charge you a fortune for it. This CD will be an excellent supplemental tool to this book. Please see our web site, www.rmcproject.com for more information.

OTHER READING MATERIAL – Most people would benefit from skimming through the book "*Principles of Project Management.*" No other material besides this book and the PMBOK® should be required. A bibliography of some useful books for those without project management training is supplied at the end of this book.

About the Author

Rita Mulcahy, PMP, is an internationally recognized expert in project management and a sought-after project management speaker, trainer, consultant, and mentor. Rita has taught over 7,000 project managers from around the world and helped thousands of people prepare for the PMP® exam. She taught the PMP® Exam Prep course for PMI® at their annual conference in 1998 and 1999 and is one of only about 15 trainers PMI® that uses to teach project management topics around the world. Rita has spoken at PMI®'s annual project management symposium to standing room only crowds for the last two years including Project World in 1999.

Rita has over 15 years and $2.5 billion of hands-on project experience on hundreds of IS, IT, new product, high-tech, service, engineering, construction, and manufacturing projects. She has been an acting PMI® chapter President and a chapter Vice President for over seven years and has taught project management courses for four major universities.

Rita heads **RMC – PROJECT MANAGEMENT**, an international project management speaking, training, consulting, and coaching firm that specializes in helping large and small companies use the latest project management tools and techniques to complete projects faster, cheaper, better, and with fewer resources. Since its founding in 1991, RMC – Project Management has worked with hundreds of IS, IT, manufacturing, Fortune 10, governments, and service firms. RMC provides the following services:

TRAINING: RMC provides customized in-house and public courses in project management. Our courses have a *"Tricks Of The Trade"* focus and include:

• PMP® Certification Training	• Determining Customer Requirements
• Project Management Fundamentals	• What Makes A Project Manager Successful?
• Risk Management	• Why Do Projects Fail and How To Prevent It
• Planning	• Tricks for Avoiding Common Project Problems
• Contracting	• Avoiding Common Stumbling Blocks in Risk
• Negotiation	• Project Management for Teams, Senior Management, Sales, and Functional Managers
• Estimating Schedule and Cost	• All PMI® PMBOK® Subjects

All our courses use the Project Management Institute's project management standards!

SPEAKING: Rita has been asked to speak around the world and has frequently been the top ranked speaker at international conferences. Recent topics include:

- 5 Ways to Improve Your Ability to Manage Projects
- What Makes a Project Manager Successful?
- Why Do Projects Fail?
- Common Project Problems and How to Avoid Them
- Avoiding Common Traps in Risk Management
- Senior Mgt.'s Role in Making Projects a Success

MENTORING: Rita has worked hands-on as a project management advisor and coach to improve the performance of teams and individuals.

CONSULTING: The list of consulting services is extensive and includes capability assessments, evaluating PM training needs, solving project problems, and improving PM methodologies.

THE EXAM

Insider Tips:

- An overview of the exam
- Types of questions on the exam
- How to study for the exam
- Tricks for passing the exam

An Overview of the Exam

Recently, PMI® completed an extensive job analysis of the work a project manager does and what they need to know to manage a project. They also completed a professional testing evaluation of the exam. As a result they not only changed the exam, they also changed how it was written. The following provide a summary of the exam, a list of what is different, and some "insider" tips on the new exam.

THE EXAM
- The exam includes 200 multiple-choice questions.

- The questions are randomly generated out of a database of hundreds of questions (e.g., a scope question followed by a risk question and a cost question).

- To pass you must get about 137 to 139 questions correct (about 68%). The minimal score depends on the complexity of the mix of questions you receive from the database of questions. There is no penalty for wrong answers.

- The exam must be completed in 4 ¼ hours. Breaks are generally allowed but extra time is not allotted for them.

APPLYING TO TAKE THE EXAM IN THE UNITED STATES OR CANADA
- PMI®'s requirements and application are available on their web site, www.pmi.org.

- PMI®'s turn around time to review your application is about 14 days. If they accept your application, you will receive a letter authorizing you to take the exam. PMI® often makes changes to the way the exam is administered. Therefore, make sure you read this letter carefully to uncover any differences from what is described here.

- Once you receive your authorization letter you can make an appointment to take the exam at one of the computerized testing centers. You must have your authorization number when you call the testing center to make an appointment. Manage your time carefully! **Once you receive your authorization letter you must take the exam within 90 days!** Sometimes the testing center may not have an opening for you to take the exam for a few weeks.

APPLYING TO TAKE THE EXAM IN OTHER COUNTRIES
- Test dates are scheduled in advance at locations around the world. In some countries the test date is only once a year. Check PMI®'s web site at www.pmi.org for your country contact person, exam dates, requirements, and application.

- In countries outside the United States and Canada, the test may be given on paper and in English, not in your native language.

© May 2000 (Registered) Rita Mulcahy, PMP at RMC – Project Management
PHONE: (612) 929-7539, EMAIL: rita@rmcproject.com, WEB: rmcproject.com

REASONS PEOPLE FAIL THE EXAM – There are many reasons why people fail the exam. I have noticed five main reasons:

1. People do not read the questions correctly.

2. They do not read all the choices.

3. They are too nervous.

4. They have not studied enough or used a source such as this book to help them.

5. They believe that they can rely exclusively on experience.

TAKING THE EXAM – This is a summary only. Please see PMI®'s web site at www.pmi.org for more details.

- You must bring your authorization letter from PMI® to the test site.

- You must bring an inexpensive, five-function calculator. If it is programmable, it will be taken away from you.

- Once you arrive at the test site, you will be given the chance to do a 15-minute computer tutorial to become familiar with the computer and its commands.

- You should also be given scrap paper, pencils, and possibly even earplugs.

- Warning: You might experience noise while taking the exam.

- You will see one question on the screen at a time. You can answer a question and/or mark it to return to it at the end

- When you finish the exam, the computer will indicate only the number of questions you answered correctly. If you pass the exam, the computer will print out a certificate and you will officially become a PMP®.

- If you do not pass the exam, PMI® will be notified and will send you information on retaking the exam. You will have to pay an additional fee to retake the exam. See PMI®'s web site (www.pmi.org) for more details.

CHANGES TO THE PMP® EXAM

- There are new "*what should you do in this situation*" type questions.

- The emphasis on the exam is based on the process of project management (project management life cycle or process groups) as follows:

PM Process	Percent of Questions	
Project Initiation	4	8
Project Planning	37	74
Project Execution	24	48
Project Control	28	56
Project Closing	7	14

- The PMBOK® and the recommended study material will not change because the exam has changed. Many old questions remain but have been reworked.

CHANGES TO THE WAY THE QUESTIONS ARE WRITTEN

- Choices of *A or B* and *never* and *always* have been removed.

- A concerted effort has been made to remove questions that give answers to other questions.

- Attempts have been made to keep all choices the same length.

- A concerted effort has been made to use "distracters." This means many of the choices will be true statements but not the answer to the question. Choices may also contain common project management errors.

- Most acronyms (WBS for work breakdown structure) should be spelled out.

- None of the correct answers should include direct quotations from the PMBOK®.

INSIGHT INTO TEST CONTENTS – Feedback from thousands of my students has provided the following insights:

- There are generally four sets of data with multiple questions related to them (see the exercise in the time section).

- There are 40 to 75 difficult "*what should you do in this situation*" type of questions.

- Most of my students feel unsure of only 50 of the 200 questions.

- Only one or two questions expect you to know the step-by-step PMBOK® processes. Only 8 or 10 questions expect you to know the inputs or outputs from the PMBOK® (see PMBOK® pages 33 and 60).

- There have been only four or five calculations on the exam for the past four years.

- There have been only four or five earned value questions (not all of them are calculations) on the exam for the past three years.

- My students have needed only 2 ½ hours to finish the exam and an additional 1½ hours to review their answers.

ANSWERING TEST QUESTIONS – The key to answering PMI®'s questions is to:

1) Know the material cold.

2) Have experience using all the project management techniques in the workplace.

3) Read the PMBOK®.

4) Understand the areas PMI® emphasizes (PMI®-isms, explained later in this book).

5) Be familiar with the types of questions.

6) Be familiar with the types of ambiguous questions.

7) Be able to pick from two answers that seem correct to you.

Types Of Questions on the Exam

Many people ask me what the questions on the test are like. Here is my summary of the types of questions you will see on the exam. Be prepared for these types of questions so you will not be upset when you see an "out of the blue" question.

1. **WHAT DO YOU DO IN THIS SITUATION TYPE QUESTIONS** – These questions require that you have "been there."

   You receive notification that a major item you are purchasing for a project will be delayed. What do you do?
   A) Ignore it. It will go away.
   B) Notify your boss.
   C) Let the customer know about it and talk over options.
   D) Meet with the team and identify alternatives.

2. **EXTRANEOUS INFORMATION** – It is very important to realize that not all the information given to you in a question must be used to answer the question. Here the numbers are extraneous.

   Experience shows that each time you double the production of widgets, unit costs decrease by 10%. Based on this, the company determines that production of 3,000 widgets should cost US $21,000. This case illustrates:
   A) Learning curve effects
   B) Law of diminishing returns
   C) 80/20 rule
   D) Parametric cost estimating
   E) A and D

3. **OUT OF THE BLUE QUESTIONS** – No matter how well you study, there will ALWAYS be questions where you have no idea what the question is asking. Here is an example.

   The concept of "optimal quality level is reached at the point where the incremental revenue from product improvement equals the incremental cost to secure it" comes from:
   A) Quality control analysis
   B) Marginal analysis
   C) Standard quality analysis
   D) Conformance analysis

4. **WORDS YOU NEVER HEARD OF** – Sometimes words that you have never seen before are used as possible choices. How many of you know that a "perk" is an abbreviation for "perquisites."

   Parking spaces, corner offices, and access to the executive dining room are examples of:
   A) Perquisites
   B) Overhead
   C) Herzberg's "motivators"
   D) Entitlements

5. **WHERE UNDERSTANDING IS IMPORTANT** – In order to answer many of the questions on the exam you must understand all the topics. Memorization is not enough!

The process of decomposing deliverables into smaller more manageable components is complete when:
   A) Project justification has been established.
   B) Change requests have occurred.
   C) Cost and duration estimates can be developed for each work element at this detail.
   D) Each work element is found in the WBS dictionary.

6. **NEW APPROACH TO KNOWN TOPIC** – There will be many instances where you understand the topic but have never thought about it in the way the question describes.

In a matrix organization, information dissemination is most likely to be effective when:
   A) Information flows both horizontally and vertically.
   B) The communication flows are kept simple.
   C) There is an inherent logic in the type of matrix chosen.
   D) Project managers and functional managers socialize.

ANSWERS:
1 D
2 E
3 B
4 A
5 C
6 A

How to Study for the Exam

There are many ways to study for an exam and many different tricks for studying quickly and efficiently. Some people study by writing and rewriting things they need to know. Some study by saying things out loud. Others study simply by reading. These methods all work but there may be a faster and more efficient method for you. After working with many people, I have perfected what my students say is the most efficient and shortest process for studying for the exam! Please consider this method before you determine how you will study.

THE MAGIC THREE – Studies have shown that if you visit a topic three times you will remember it. Therefore, you should read this book and take the sample exam three times before you take the exam.

BE IN TEST TAKING MODE – To be prepared to take the exam, you need to be familiar with the exam topics but you also must be in test taking mode. Do not underestimate the physical aspects of taking an exam for 4 ½ hours. The last question you answer is just as important as the first one. Study the material. Also, to practice being in the test environment, take the sample tests for over 4 hours and keep track of the time it takes you to answer the 200 exam questions.

AN EFFICIENT STEP BY STEP PROCESS

1. Before you review the materials, take all the sample exams in this book in one sitting - like the actual exam.

2. Do not analyze your right and wrong answers at this point. Just list the chapters beginning with the chapter with the most errors and ending with the chapter with the least errors. This will give you an indication of the chapters that are most difficult for you and help you determine an overall study plan. It will also help you determine if you really do know project management and how much studying you will need.

3. Read the material for the first time, focusing on the chapters with the most errors.

4. If it is at all possible, form a study group. This will actually make your study time more effective and shorter! You will be able to ask someone questions and the studying (and celebrating afterward) will be more fun. A study group consists of only three or four people, no more and no less.

   Meet with a study group and pick someone to lead the discussion of each chapter (preferably someone who is **not** comfortable with the chapter). Each time you meet, depending on your level of knowledge, either go over the sample exams or ask each other questions about topics you do not understand, or both. Most groups meet for one hour per chapter.

   - NOTE: This book is written for individual use because it includes exercises and activities. Each member of the study group will need their own copy.

5. Either independently or with the group, further research questions you did not understand or answered incorrectly. If you find it necessary, review other relevant material or read the books listed in the bibliography at the end of this book.

6. If possible, retake the sample test in one sitting like the exam.

7. Read this book and take the sample exam at least three times, until you pass all the questions.

Tricks For Taking the Exam

1. A major trick to answering PMI®'s questions is to first try to answer the question from PMI®'s perspective and not the perspective you have acquired from your life experience. If that does not give you an answer, rely on your training and life experience, in that order.

2. Another major trick is to first read only the question. Note the topics discussed in the question and the descriptors (e.g. except, includes, not an example of). This should help you understand what the question is asking. Determine what your answer should be and <u>then</u> look at the answers.

3. One of the main reasons people answer incorrectly is because they do not read all four choices. Do not make the same mistake! Practice reading the questions and all four choices when you take the sample exams.

4. As soon as you are given paper at the exam, write down all the formulas and major processes.

5. Write down things that you do not know as you take the exam. You may see other questions that help you figure out the meaning of what you do not know.

6. Visit the exam site before the test to see how long it will take you to get there and to see what the testing room looks like. This is particularly helpful if you are a nervous test taker.

7. During the exam, mark the questions you are unsure of and then use any extra time at the end to go back to them.

8. Look for the "rah, rah" answer. (e.g., The project manager is so important. The WBS is so useful.)

9. Take the night off before the exam and do something relaxing. Read a book or watch a movie. DO NOT STUDY! You will need time to process all you have learned so you can remember it when you take the exam.

10. Make sure you are comfortable during the exam. Wear layered clothing and bring a sweater to sit on in case the chairs are uncomfortable.

11. Bring snacks! Bring lunch! Food may not be available if you get hungry. You may not be able to bring snacks into the exam room but they will be available just outside the room.

12. Use deep breathing techniques to help relax. The more oxygen you inhale, the clearer your mind. This is particularly helpful if you are very nervous before or during the exam.

13. Use all the exam time. Do not leave early unless you have reviewed each question twice.

14. Prepare a test taking technique and stick to it. This may mean, "I will take a 10 minute break after every 50 questions because I get tired quickly," or "I will answer all the questions as quickly as possible and then take a break and review my answers."

15. It is okay to change your answers as long as you have a good reason.

16. Eliminate incorrect answers to improve your probability of selecting the correct one.

17. Practice being able to pick from two seemingly "right" answers.

18. When a question asks you to fill in a blank space, the correct answer may not be grammatically correct when inserted in the sentence.

THE MATERIALS

Review,
Insider Tips,
Exercises,
Games, and
Activities

Chapter 1

Recurring Themes:
PMI®-isms

One of the side objectives of any certification exam is to continuously expand the base of industry knowledge. If there are areas where certain fundamentals are lacking, and this is certainly true in project management, the certification exam will most likely emphasize them. PMI® does the same. I call these PMI®-isms.

PMI®-isms are not stressed and sometimes not even mentioned in the PMBOK®, yet you must know and understand them for the exam! In many instances, identifying PMI®-isms should help you pick the right answer from what seems like two correct answers.

A summary list of commonly used PMI®-isms (which the rest of my book describes in detail) is included here:

- HISTORICAL RECORDS should be collected and used as a basis for planning, estimating, and risk.

- PMI® stresses kickoff meetings but their definition may be different than yours.

    A meeting of all parties to the project (customers, contractors, project team, senior management, agencies, functional management) held just before beginning work on the project at the end of the Planning Phase.

    This is a communication and coordination meeting to make sure everyone is familiar with the details of the project and the people working on the project.

    Specific topics at this meeting depend on the nature of the project and the people involved. Topics may include communication plans, setting up meetings, discussing potential problems, etc.

- Work Breakdown Structures (WBS) are "wonderful" and should be used on every project.

- Project managers are "wonderful," "great," and must be very skilled (a rah! rah! for project management topic).

- PMI® does not approve of gold plating (the statement as well as the concept).

- The needs of all stakeholders should be taken into account on all projects.

- The team member must be involved in project planning, not just told what the task is and how long they have to complete it.

- The project manager must be pro-active. Although PMI® does not use this word, correct answers indicate that the project manager must find problems early, look for changes, prevent problems, etc.

Chapter 2

Project Management Framework
(PMBOK® Chapters 1-3)

These chapters provide the foundation for project management and convey some important concepts. Most of the questions are easy but watch out for questions about weak or strong matrices as explained below. Make sure you memorize concepts, definitions, and approaches. Make sure you read these chapters of the PMBOK® at least once.

HOT TOPICS, in order of importance:

- Life cycle
  - Project life cycle
  - Project management life cycle
- Organizational theory
  - Matrix
    - Strong
    - Weak
    - Balanced
    - Tight
  - Project expeditor
  - Project coordinator
  - Functional
  - Projectized
- Definition of a project
- Definition of a program
- Stakeholder
- Stakeholder Management

DEFINITION OF A PROJECT (page 4, all page number references are to the PMBOK®):
You must know the definition of a project.
1. *Temporary* endeavor with a beginning and an end
2. Creates a *unique* product or service
3. Done for a *purpose*
4. Has *interrelated activities*

DEFINITION OF A PROGRAM (page 8): "A program is a group of projects..."

STAKEHOLDER and **STAKEHOLDER MANAGEMENT** (page 15): PMI® defines stakeholders as:
- Project Manager
- Customer
- Performing organization, owners, government agencies
- Sponsor
- Team
- Internal/external
- End user
- Society, citizens
- Others: owners, funders, suppliers, contractors

"The project management team must identify the stakeholders, determine their needs and expectations, and manage and influence those expectations to ensure a successful project." The key to customer satisfaction is careful and accurate needs analysis. Therefore stakeholder management is a proactive task. The project manager should not just receive a scope of work and then strive to complete it but rather determine all the stakeholders and incorporate their needs into the project. Make sure you understand this subtle difference, especially if your projects are managed differently!

LIFE CYCLE: (pages 11-15 and pages 27-35): There are two different "life cycles" that you should be very familiar with:

PROJECT LIFE CYCLE (pages 11-15). This life cycle describes what technical work needs to be done on the project and may have the following phases. Other phases are listed in the PMBOK®. Questions about this life cycle are not often part of the exam.

CONSTRUCTION – feasibility, planning, design, production, turnover, and startup.

INFORMATION SYSTEMS – requirement analysis, high-level design, detailed design, coding, testing, installation, conversion, and operation.

PROJECT MANAGEMENT LIFE CYCLE (process areas, pages 27-35). The Project Management Life Cycle relates to how the work is managed. There could be 40 to 60 questions throughout the exam that relate to "what do you do when." These questions, though frequent, are relatively easy as long as you <u>pay attention to this area</u>. The chart below translates PMBOK® pages 27-35 into the real world, which is what the exam is all about.

Initiation	Planning	Execution	Control	Close-out
Feasibility	Scope statement	Executing the project plan	Overall change control	Procurement audits
High-level planning	Create a project team	Complete work packages or tasks	Performance reporting	Product verification
Charter	Work breakdown structure (WBS)	Information distribution	Scope control	Formal acceptance
	WBS dictionary	Quality assurance	Quality control	Lessons learned
	Finalize the team	Team development	Risk response control	Update records
	Network diagram	Scope verification	Schedule control	Archive records
	Estimate time and cost	Progress meetings	Cost control	Release team
	Critical path		Manage by exception to the project plan	
	Schedule			
	Budget			
	Procurement plan			
	Quality plan			
	Risk identification, quantification and response development			
	Change control plan			
	Communication plan			
	Management plan			
	Final project plan			
	Project plan approval			
	Kickoff meeting			

Overall
Influencing the organization
Leading
Problem solving
Negotiating
Communicating
Meetings

Pages 27 and 28 in the PMBOK® discuss project management process areas. These process areas can be loosely equated to a project management life cycle except that they are also applicable to each phase of the project life cycle (see PMBOK® page 29 figure 3-3.) The process areas overlap over the life of the project (see PMBOK® page 29 figure 3-2.)

Some of the items listed in the chart in one column, such as team development and influencing the organization, are really done throughout the project. Do not let the chart change your common sense about when such activities, and any others, should be done. The exam expects you to know that team building (included in team development) starts at the beginning of a project and does not stop until closure. You will also note that a few of the Core and Facilitating Processes noted in the PMBOK® are not listed here because projects do not always address these topics during the part of the project management life cycle listed in the PMBOK®.

For the exam you should know what each term means, the phase of the project management life cycle when each should be done, and the specific order of the planning phase. In looking at this chart you will note that the planning phase has a specific order that only becomes iterative when you get to the "plans."

Please note that there are many terms that could be placed in more than one phase. The chart lists the terms in the Phase where they are most frequently done. Read pages 27-35 in the PMBOK® but make sure you memorize the chart. When you are ready, play the Life Cycle Game on the subsequent pages.

Life Cycle Game

INSTRUCTIONS: The following pages contain the phases and activities of the project management life cycle (a shorter version of the list on the previous page). Cut them out and practice putting them into the correct Phase on your own or in a group. Then, when you think they are all in the correct Phase, put planning in order. Lastly check your answers to the chart on the previous page.

NOTE: Only the Planning Phase has a defined order. You should be able to put planning in order in your sleep.

I have said that you must know project management to pass the test. If you find you do not know many of the items listed or why there is an order to planning, you might consider project management training before taking the exam. These topics will all be included in the exam.

CREATE A PROJECT TEAM	FINAL PROJECT PLAN
PROJECT PLAN APPROVAL	MANAGE BY EXCEPTION TO THE PLAN
MANAGEMENT PLAN	FINALIZE THE PROJECT TEAM
RISK IDENTIFICATION, QUANTIFICATION AND RESPONSE DEVELOPMENT	SCOPE VERIFICATION
PROCUREMENT AUDITS	PERFORMANCE REPORTING

CHARTER	LESSONS LEARNED
SCOPE STATEMENT	PROBLEM SOLVING
WORK BREAKDOWN STRUCTURE	CRITICAL PATH
RISK RESPONSE CONTROL	NETWORK DIAGRAM
BUDGET	SCHEDULE

ESTIMATE TIME AND COST	OVERALL CHANGE CONTROL
COMMUNICATING	LEADING
RELEASE TEAM	KICK OFF MEETING
PRODUCT VERIFICATION	PROGRESS MEETINGS
WBS DICTIONARY	CHANGE CONTROL PLAN

INITIATION	TEAM DEVELOPMENT
PLANNING	QUALITY ASSURANCE
EXECUTION	QUALITY CONTROL
CONTROL	INFORMATION DISTRIBUTION
CLOSE-OUT	COMPLETE WORK PACKAGES

COMMUNICATION PLAN	FEASIBILITY
FORMAL ACCEPTANCE	HIGH LEVEL PLANNING
UPDATE RECORDS	INFLUENCING THE ORGANIZATION
SCOPE CONTROL	SCHEDULE CONTROL
QUALITY PLAN	COST CONTROL

EXECUTE THE PROJECT PLAN	ARCHIVE RECORDS
PROCUREMENT PLAN	NEGOTIATING
MEETINGS	OVERALL

ORGANIZATIONAL THEORY (*Principles of Project Management* pages 11-22, PMBOK® pages 18 – 22): Organizational theory describes how a company can be organized to get its work completed. PMI® talks about five types of organizational structure. Each type is described in terms of the level of authority of the project manager. Many people have said that they wished they had spent more time studying this topic. Questions on the exam related to organizational theory include:

- Who has the power in each type of organization, project manager or functional manager
- Advantages of each type of organization
- Disadvantages of each type of organization

FUNCTIONAL – This is the most common form of organization. The organization is set up within different functional areas (e.g., accounting, marketing, and manufacturing).

A functional organizational chart might look like this:

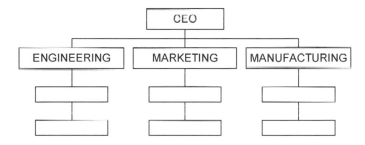

NOTE: Many questions on the exam ask questions about the other forms of organization compared to functional. Sometimes the reference to the functional form of organization is not even stated. Please see the first sample question at the end of this chapter.

PROJECT EXPEDITOR – In this form of organization, the project expeditor acts primarily as a staff assistant and communication coordinator. The expeditor cannot personally make or enforce decisions. This form of organization may look like this:

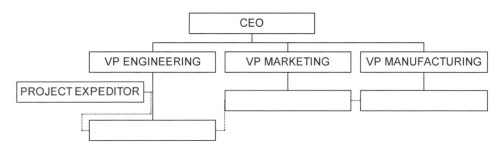

PROJECT COORDINATOR – This form of organization is similar to the Project Expeditor except the coordinator has some power to make decisions, has some authority, and reports to a higher-level manager. This form may look like this:

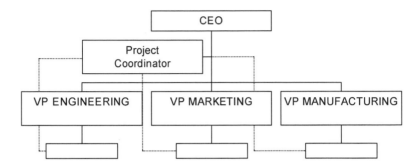

MATRIX – This form is an attempt to maximize the strengths and weaknesses of both the Functional and the Project forms but has people report to **two bosses**. Most of the questions relating to organizational forms should be about the matrix organization. This form may look like this:

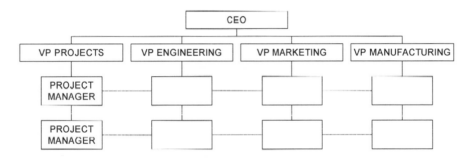

Expect questions that ask about the advantages and disadvantages of each form of organization. Most of those questions relate to the matrix form.

Strong Matrix – The balance of power rests with the project manager.

Weak Matrix – The balance of power rests with the functional manager.

Balanced Matrix – The power is balanced between the functional and project managers.

Tight Matrix – Watch out for this topic! It has nothing to do with a matrix organization. It simply refers to locating the project team's offices in the same room. You can expect to see this listed on the exam on many of the matrix organization questions! Watch out!

PROJECTIZED – All organization is by projects. The project manager has total control of projects. Personnel are assigned and report to a project manager.

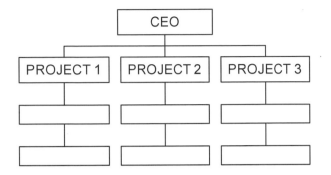

Exercise:

<u>INSTRUCTIONS</u>: Test yourself! List the advantages and disadvantages of each organizational form in the spaces provided below.

PROJECTIZED

Advantages	Disadvantages

MATRIX

Advantages	Disadvantages

FUNCTIONAL

Advantages	Disadvantages

Answer: Some potential answers are listed below. Remember that many of the answers should include the phrase "as compared to functional:"

PROJECTIZED

Advantages	Disadvantages
Efficient project organization	No "home" when project is completed
Loyalty to the project	Lack of professionalism in disciplines
More effective communication than functional	Duplication of facilities and job functions
	Less efficient use of resources

MATRIX

Advantages	Disadvantages
Highly visible project objectives	Not cost effective because of extra administrative personnel
Improved project manager control over resources	More than one boss for project teams
More support from functional organizations	More complex to monitor and control
Maximum utilization of scarce resources	Tougher resource allocation problems
Better coordination	Extensive policies and procedures needed
Better horizontal and vertical dissemination of information than functional	Functional managers may have different priorities than project managers
People maintain "a home"	Higher potential for duplication of effort and conflict

FUNCTIONAL

Advantages	Disadvantages
Easier management of specialists	People place more emphasis on this functional specialty
People report to only one supervisor	No career path in project management

SAMPLE QUESTIONS
Framework Management

3rd Time	2nd Time	1st Time

1) One of the main advantages of a matrix organization is:
   A. Improved project manager control over resources
   B. More than one boss for project teams
   C. Communication is easier
   D. Reporting is easier

2) A project expeditor is different than a project coordinator because he/she:
   A. Can make no decisions
   B. Can make more decisions
   C. Reports to a higher-level manager
   D. Has some authority

3) In a projectized organization, the project team:
   A. Reports to many bosses
   B. Has loyalty to the project
   C. Will not always have a home
   D. B and C

4) The final project budget is created during which life cycle phase:
   A. Initiation
   B. It is given to the project manager before the project management life cycle
   C. Planning
   D. Execution

5) The project charter is created during which life cycle phase:
   A. Execution
   B. Planning
   C. Closeout
   D. Initiation

6) Projects have the least attention in what form of organization:
   A. Functional
   B. Matrix
   C. Expeditor
   D. Coordinator

7) A project stakeholder may include:
   A. End users
   B. Suppliers
   C. Citizens
   D. All of the above

© May 2000 (Registered) Rita Mulcahy, PMP at RMC – Project Management
PHONE: (612) 929-7539, EMAIL: rita@rmcproject.com, WEB: rmcproject.com

8) Bob has very tittle project experience but he has been assigned as the project manager of a new project. Because he will be working in a matrix organization to complete his project, he can expect communications to be:
   A. Simple
   B. Open and accurate
   C. Complex
   D. Hard to automate

9) You are a project manager for a new building design project and have just received a project charter. You can create a detailed project schedule only after?
   A. A project plan is created
   B. A WBS is created
   C. A budget is created
   D. A project control plan is created

10) A project sponsor has been holding team meetings during project planning to get a project underway. Then the company hires a new project manager for the project. Who should be in control of the project during project planning?
   A. The project manager
   B. The team member
   C. Functional manager
   D. The project manager's boss

11) A project team member is talking to another team member and complaining that so many people are asking him to do things. If he works in a functional organization, who has the power?
   A. The project manager
   B. The functional manager
   C. The team
   D. None of the above

12) Who has more power in a projectized organization?
   A. The project manager
   D. The functional manager
   C. The team
   D. None of the above

13) Which of the following is not a characteristic of a project?
   A. Temporary
   B. Definite beginning and an end
   C. Interrelated activities
   D. Repeats itself every month

14) Which of the following is not part of the team's stakeholder management effort?
   A. Give them extras
   B. Identify them
   C. Determine their needs and expectations
   D. Manage their expectations

© May 2000 (Registered) Rita Mulcahy, PMP at RMC – Project Management
PHONE: (612) 929-7539, EMAIL: rita@rmcproject.com, WEB: rmcproject.com

ANSWERS:
1 A
2 A
3 D
4 C
5 D
6 A
7 D
8 C
9 B
10 A
11 B
12 A
13 D
14 A

Chapter 3

Integration Management

(PMBOK® Chapter 4)

Integration is all about putting the pieces of the project together into a cohesive whole. This may include trading off among the different project objectives, project plan development and execution, and change control. Integration is primarily the role of the project manager because the project manager is the only one responsible for seeing the overall project "big picture." Only a few questions about integration are on the exam, and these questions are easy.

HOT TOPICS, in order of importance, are:

- The project manager as integrator
- Historical records
- Project Plan
- Overall change control
- Change control system
- Lessons Learned
- Stakeholder management
- Work authorization system
- Change control board
- Configuration management
- Project management information system
- Meetings

THE ROLE OF THE PROJECT MANAGER AS INTEGRATOR: While it is the role of the team members to complete their piece of the pie (project), it is the project manager's role to integrate all the pieces into a whole. Management stands behind the project, helps define the pie, and protects it from changes. These roles are illustrated in the following graphic.

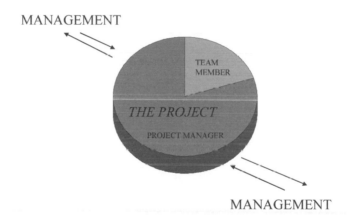

HISTORICAL RECORDS (page 40 and throughout the PMBOK®): Historical records (or data) are needed in order to do much of project management well and may take the form of past project:

- Files
- Lessons Learned
- Actual costs
- Time estimates
- WBS's
- Benchmarks
- Risks

Most companies do not have a database of historical records. This leaves the project manager to constantly plan, estimate, and schedule projects from scratch. The creation of a database of historical records is an organizational responsibility that can result in major inputs to continuous improvement. Because there is a lack of such data, PMI® should mention it many times on the exam.

THE PROJECT PLAN (page 42): A Project Plan is created by the team, not just the project manager or management. You must know what goes into a Project Plan.

Exercise:

INSTRUCTIONS: Test yourself! Make a list of the items that go into a Project Plan in the spaces provided below.

Answer: Some things that may go into a project plan (see also bullets on PMBOK® page 42).

Project charter	Major milestones
Scope statement	Key staff
WBS	Change control plan/system
Budget	Management and communication plan
Schedule	Procurement plan
Risks	Quality plan

OVERALL CHANGE CONTROL (page 44): The PMBOK® says that the project manager must be concerned with:

1. Influencing the factors that affect change
2. Ensuring that the change is beneficial
3. Determining that a change has occurred
4. Managing changes as they occur.

Think about this list for a moment. How does it differ from your projects? Although much can be said about all four of these items, the first one is the most confusing. Most people think it is the project manager's job is simply to make changes. In fact, the project manager should determine all the factors that can cause changes to the project and then pro-actively use his or her influence to prevent them from occurring. For example, if the project manager discovers that the scope of work is incomplete, he or she should try to influence those responsible for completing the scope of work before project planning begins.

The exam has many situational questions. Many of the situational questions deal with how to make change. For example:

A functional manager wants to make a change to the project. What is the first thing a project manager should do? Or a senior manager wants to make a change to the scope of work. What is the best thing to do first?

The answers are the same in either case. Evaluate the impact of the change to the project. Then meet with the team to discuss alternatives before making a decision to use project reserves and meet with management. The exam often lists some common but incorrect choices such as meet with the customer first or meet with management first. All changes must be evaluated before a decision can be reached.

CHANGE CONTROL SYSTEM (page 45): A collection of formal, documented procedures, paperwork, tracking systems and approval levels for authorizing changes. A change control system includes both hard (procedures) and soft (software, management practices) aspects. It may include any of the following:

- A change control plan included in the project plan outlining how changes will be managed.
- Creation of change control board to approve all changes (see below)
- Change control procedures – how, who
- Performance statistics (e.g., time/system, time/drawing)
- Reports (e.g., software output, milestone charts, resource usage)
- Change forms
- Specification reviews
- Demonstrations
- Testing
- Meetings
- Plans for taking corrective action

CHANGE CONTROL BOARD (page 45): A change control board is usually a group of people from the organization that is formed to approve or reject project changes. The board must approve a change before it can be executed.

CONFIGURATION MANAGEMENT (page 45): This term has many definitions depending on the industry. For the purposes of the exam, think of this as rigorous change management as it relates to scope. It is therefore a subset of the change control system.

WORK AUTHORIZATION SYSTEM (page 43): "A formal procedure for sanctioning project work to ensure that work is done at the right time and in the right sequence." It is also a method to control "gold plating," such as the provision of an extra functionality or service. It defines what the task is and is not and may take the form of a WBS dictionary (see a later description).

MEETINGS: The project manager may have many different types of meetings. Meetings are a problem in the real world in that many project managers manage by meeting and that most meetings are not efficient. You can have questions on who should attend meetings (only those that need to be there), about keeping meeting minutes and the different types of meetings (team meetings, customer meetings, problem solving meetings.) There may also be some questions which require you to realize that you can determine project status in ways that do not require status meetings.

PROJECT MANAGEMENT INFORMATION SYSTEM (page 42): The combination of a manual and an automated system to let the project manager know the status of all project tasks. This is one way to determine status instead of just relying on meetings. A project management information system may include:

- Meetings
- Asking questions
- Use of a Gantt chart

LESSONS LEARNED: This is a topic that is only briefly mentioned at the end of each chapter in the PMBOK®, yet it has great importance in real project management. I will only discuss it here.

A Lessons Learned is done during the Closeout Phase of the project. PMI®'s philosophy is that the project is not complete until a Lessons Learned is completed. Lessons are not learned and no continuous improvement can occur without a Lessons Learned.

A good Lessons Learned covers "what have we done and how can we do it better" and addresses three areas:

1. The technical aspects of the project
2. Project management (How did we do with WBS creation, risk, etc.?)
3. Management (How did we do with communication and leadership as a project manager?)

At the very least, the project manager completes the Lessons Learned. Better yet, the whole project team completes it. Even better, it is completed by the whole team and made available throughout the company. A Lessons Learned is sometimes called a "post mortem."

SAMPLE QUESTIONS
Integration Management

	3rd Time	2nd Time	1st Time

1) Effective project integration usually requires an emphasis on:
- A. The personal careers of the team members
- B. Timely updates to the Project Plan
- C. Effective communications at key interface points
- D. Internal control

2) The need for _____ is one of the major driving forces for communication in a project.
- A. Optimization
- B. Integrity
- C. Integration
- D. Differentiation

3) Historical records are used for:
- A. Estimating
- B. Risk management
- C. Project planning
- D. All of the above

4) When it comes to changes, the project manager's attention is best spent on:
- A. Handling changes when they come to light
- B. Recording changes
- C. Letting management know about changes
- D. Preventing unnecessary changes

5) Management's role on a project is to:
- A. Help plan tasks
- B. Help prevent changes to the project objectives
- C. Discuss the technical issues
- D. Help put the project plan together

6) A project manager is creating a project plan and he and the project sponsor are arguing about what needs to be done to control changes to the project. Which of the following is not part of an effective change control system?
- A. Procedures
- B. Standards for reports
- C. Meetings
- D. Lessons learned

7) A work authorization system is used to:
   A. Control who does each task
   B. Control gold plating
   C. Let management know what tasks are planned
   D. Let functional managers know what tasks are planned

8) A project is plagued by changes to the project charter. The person with primary responsibility to decide what changes are necessary is _____.
   A. Project manager
   B. Team
   C. Management
   D. Stakeholder

9) Integration is done by:
   A. Project manager
   B. Team
   C. Management
   D. Stakeholder

10) Integration means?
   A. Familiarizing team members with the project
   B. Putting all the pieces of a project into a cohesive whole
   C. Putting all the pieces of a project into a program
   D. Assigning all team members to teams

11) All technical work is completed on the project. Which of the following remains to be done?
   A. A project budget
   B. A risk management plan
   C. A staff management plan
   D. A Lessons learned

12) A Lessons Learned is used for:
   A. Historical records for future projects
   B. A planning record for the current project
   C. Telling the team all the good things the project manager has done
   D. Telling the team the project plan

13) During the execution of a project the project manager determines that a change is needed to material purchased for the project. The project manager calls a meeting of the team to plan how to make the change. This is an example of:
   A. Management by objectives
   B. Lack of a change control system
   C. Good team relations
   D. Lack of a clear work breakdown structure

14) A lessons learned is completed by:
   A.   The project manager
   B.   The team
   C.   Management
   D.   Stakeholders

15) A project stakeholder is known to make many changes during the projects that involve them. If this person is one of the project stakeholders on a new project, what should a project manager do in this situation?
   A.   Not allow the stakeholder to make changes
   B.   Get stakeholder involvement during project planning
   C.   Talk to the stakeholder's boss
   D.   Complain to management about the stakeholders past activities

16) You are a new project manager who has never managed a project before and you have been asked to plan a new project. It would be best in this situation to rely on _____ during planning in order to improve your chance of success?
   A.   Your intuition
   B.   Your training
   C.   Historical records
   D.   Responsibility charts

17) A project plan consists of:
   A.   A printout from project management software
   B.   A Gantt chart
   C.   Risk, staff, change control, budget, and other plans
   D.   The project scope of work

18) A project manager discovers during planning that part of the scope of work is undefined. They should:
   A.   Continue to plan the project because the scope of work is not ready
   B.   Do what they can to get the scope of work defined
   C.   Wait until the scope of work is defined and issue a change to the project
   D.   Complain to management

19) Which of the following is NOT part of administrative closeout?
   A.   Lessons Learned
   B.   Formal acceptance
   C.   Reduced resource spending
   D.   Benefit-cost analysis

ANSWERS:

1 C
2 C
3 D
4 D
5 B
6 D
7 B
8 C
9 A
10 B
11 D
12 A
13 B
14 B
15 B
16 C
17 C
18 B
19 C

Chapter 4

Scope Management
(PMBOK® Chapter 5)

Scope management covers many important aspects of project management. Many project managers have never completed a Charter or Work Breakdown Structure on their projects nor are they familiar with project selection techniques. With real-world experience in these areas, scope questions are easy.

<table>
<tr><td valign="top">

HOT TOPICS, in order of importance, are:

- Work Breakdown Structure (WBS)
- Scope definition and decomposition
- Project charter
- Project selection criteria
- Scope verification
- Definition of scope management
- WBS dictionary
- Delphi technique
- Management By Objectives (MBO)
- Please see the **PMBOK** for:
  - Constraints
  - Corrective action
  - Scope of work

</td><td valign="top">

THE WORK BREAKDOWN STRUCTURE (WBS, page 54 - 55): This is one of the biggest areas of PMI®-ism because it is one of the key tools of project management that is not known by many people who manage projects. In order to answer questions about the WBS, you must understand the following and have created one in the workplace. The questions that deal with "what do you do in this situation" can be very difficult if you have never completed a WBS for a real project. If you are familiar with the following information and have created a WBS in the workplace, questions that deal with the WBS should be easy.

A WBS is a "deliverable oriented grouping of project ~~elements~~ components which organizes and defines the total scope of the project." It breaks the project into smaller and more manageable pieces. Smart project managers know that they cannot manage a project, they need to manage the pieces. Although the WBS may look like a corporate organizational chart, it is not!

</td></tr>
</table>

Did you Know
A Work Breakdown Structure looks like this: **not this:**

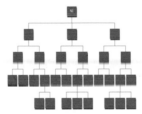

Exercise: Do you really know what a Work Breakdown Structure is?

<u>INSTRUCTIONS</u>: Test yourself! The chart on the right is a list of tasks on a Gantt chart and the one on the left is a real WBS. Describe the difference between the two charts in the space provided below.

Answer: The one on the right…

Does not break down the project into smaller, more manageable pieces.
May include large and small tasks that are greater than the 80-hour rule of thumb.
May not include all the work. (In contrast, the construction of the WBS chart on the left helps to ensure that nothing slips through the cracks.)
Does not help to get your mind around the project.
Is usually not created by the team.
Does not show a complete hierarchy of the project, even with indentation.
Does not result in a clear understanding of the project by all and does not result in project buy-in.

The creation of a WBS has only a few "rules":

- The first level is most commonly the same as the project life cycle (requirement analysis, design, coding, testing, conversion, and operation).
- The first level is completed before the project is broken down further.
- Each level of the WBS is a smaller segment of the level above.
- The entire project is included in each of the highest levels. However, eventually some levels will be broken down further than others.
- Work towards the project deliverables.
- Break down the project into tasks, work packages or activities that:

    Are realistically and confidently estimable

    Cannot be logically subdivided further

    Can be completed quickly (under 80 hours is a rule of thumb)

    Have a meaningful conclusion and deliverable

    Can be completed without interruption (without the need for more information)

On most projects, the phrase "work packages" relates to project tasks or activities. On large projects, the project manager may manage the project only to the work package level, leaving the work packages to be broken into tasks by the team members. On the exam, be careful to interpret and identify which situation the question is referring to.

The WBS is the foundation of the project. It provides the foundation for all project planning, and project control.

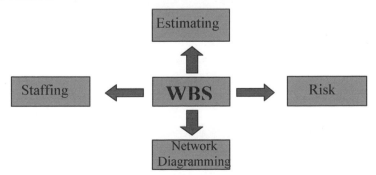

Exercise:

: Test yourself! What are the benefits of using a WBS?

Answer: The benefits of using a WBS are that it:

- Helps prevent work slipping through the cracks
- Provides the project team with an understanding of where their pieces fit into the overall Project Plan and gives them an indication of the impact of their work on the project as a whole
- Facilitates communication and cooperation between and among the project team and stakeholders
- Helps prevent changes
- Focuses the team's experience into what needs to be done, resulting in a higher quality and easier project
- Provides a basis for estimating staff, cost, and time
- Provides PROOF of need for staff, cost, and time
- Gets team buy-in and builds the team
- Helps get your mind around the project
- Helps new team members see their role

Tip – Phrases about the WBS that have been answers on the exam:
- Graphical picture of the hierarchy of the project
- Identifies all tasks
- Foundation on which the project is built
- Is VERY important
- Forces you to think through all aspects of the project
- A WBS can be re-used for other projects

SCOPE DEFINITION AND DECOMPOSITION (pages 52-54): Some students confuse these terms with the WBS. The PMBOK® defines scope definition and decomposition as "subdividing the major project deliverables into smaller, more manageable components." The best way to handle these terms is to think of scope definition and decomposition as WHAT you are doing, and the WBS as the TOOL to do it. (Scope definition and decomposition have only been on the exam occasionally over the last few years, so do not worry!)

PROJECT CHARTER (page 50): This is another minor area of PMI®-ism. The exam could include up to five questions that reference a project charter. You should know what a project charter is and why it is important to the project manager. Keep in mind that PMI®'s definition of a charter may be different than yours!

Exercise:

INSTRUCTIONS: Test yourself! Answer the questions below.

What is included in a project charter?	What does the charter do for the project manager?

Answer – Part I:

A project charter may look like this:

PROJECT CHARTER

PROJECT TITLE AND DESCRIPTION: (Briefly describe the project.)

PROJECT MANAGER ASSIGNED AND AUTHORITY LEVEL: (name, can he or she determine budget, schedule, staffing, etc.?)

GOALS AND OBJECTIVES: (Describe in detail what the project is to accomplish, include numbers whenever possible.)

BUSINESS CASE: (Why is the project being done?)

PRODUCT DESCRIPTION: (When the project is completed, specifically what is wanted? For example, is it a new system that performs at a certain speed or a report of a certain length and content. Be specific!)

SIGNED AND APPROVED BY:

_____

SENIOR MANAGEMENT: (A person who is high enough in the organization to warrant everyone on the team reporting to him or her)

ANSWER – Part II:

The Charter provides the following benefits:

- Gives the project manager authority.
  On the exam, this is the most commonly described benefit or use of the Charter. In most project situations, the project team does not report to the project manager in the corporate structure. This leads to issues of "how to gain cooperation and performance."
- Formally recognizes the existence of the project or establishes the project.
  This means that the project does not exist without a Charter.
- Provides the objectives of the project.
  Most project managers are not provided with the basic information (what is in the Charter) to complete the project. The information provided in the Charter is considered vital to the success of the project. Without the Charter information, it is like being told to get into a car and drive without being told where to go.

The project charter is also:

- Created by a manager who is external and higher in the corporate hierarchy, not the project manager or the team
- Created during the Initiation Phase
- Broad enough so it does not need to change as the project changes (except under extreme conditions)

PROJECT SELECTION CRITERIA (page 50): This is another area that is given greater weight on the exam than in the PMBOK®. Although the project manager may not be involved in the selection of one project over another, you need to know that such a process occurs as well as the categories of criteria that can be used.

Two main categories of project selection methods exist:

1. Benefit measurement methods (comparative approach) – These methods compare one project to another.
   - Murder board – The project is presented to a panel of people who try to shoot it down.
   - Peer review
   - Scoring models
   - Economic models
   - Benefit compared to costs
2. Constrained optimization methods (mathematical approach) –
   - Linear programming
   - Integer programming
   - Dynamic programming
   - Multi-objective programming

A question on the exam has asked, "what type of project selection technique is linear programming?" The answer, of course, is constrained optimization, but the exam does not require you to know the definitions of linear programming, dynamic programming, or multi-objective programming!

SCOPE VERIFICATION (page 56-58): "The process of formalizing acceptance of the project scope by the stakeholders. It requires reviewing work products and results to ensure that all are completed correctly and satisfactorily." This is customer feedback on a more detailed basis. It is done at the end of each project phase (not project management phase) and results in formal acceptance.

This is not something new, yet the questions about it on the exam can be rather vague. Make sure you read the questions clearly! One question asked for the "key aspect of scope verification." The answer does not involve the *correctness* of the work, that is quality control. The answer was "customer *acceptance* of project efforts." Note the difference!

DEFINITION OF SCOPE MANAGEMENT (page 47): "Includes the processes required to ensure that the project includes all the work and only the work required, to complete the project successfully. It is primarily concerned with controlling what is and what is not in the project."

This is one of the definitions you should know and understand for the exam. It relates to a recurring PMI®-ism that also shows up in questions relating to "gold plating" and quality. PMI® states that you should give the customer what they asked for, no more and no less. Giving any extras is a waste of time and has no benefit to the project.

PMI®'s reasoning is that what you think is an extra might in fact have no value to the customer. Considering that currently only 26 percent of all projects succeed, we should concentrate on completing the project scope of work instead of compounding the problem by adding more work. Make sure you understand these statements fully to be able to answer a wide variety of questions about scope and quality.

WBS DICTIONARY (page 56, second paragraph): Although created with the team member's assistance, a WBS Dictionary is designed to control what work is done and when. Sometimes also called a task description, it helps the project by putting a boundary on what is included in the task (or work package) and what is not included. A WBS Dictionary may be included in a work authorization system and may contain information similar to the following:

WBS DICTIONARY (Task Description)			
Project Name _____	Task No. _____	Date Issued _____	Person Assigned _____
Length _____	Due Date _____	Budget _____	Sign Off _____
Task Description			
Goals and objectives			
Product description			
Acceptance criteria			
Interdependencies: Before this task _____		After this task _____	

© May 2000 (Registered) Rita Mulcahy, PMP at RMC – Project Management
PHONE: (612) 929-7539, EMAIL: rita@rmcproject.com, WEB: rmcproject.com

DELPHI TECHNIQUE: A method most commonly used to obtain expert opinions on technical issues, the necessary scope of work, or the risks. A request for information is sent to experts, their returned responses are compiled and then sent back to them for further review. The Delphi Technique has two rules: (1) keep the experts' identities anonymous and (2) try to build consensus.

MANAGEMENT BY OBJECTIVES (MBO): A management philosophy that says an organization should be managed by objectives. It has three steps:

1. Establish unambiguous and realistic objectives
2. Periodically evaluate if objectives are being met
3. Take corrective action

You should know what this means for the project manager. If the project is not in line with or does not support the corporate objectives, then the project is likely to lose resources, assistance, and attention. You should also know that MBO works only if management supports it.

SAMPLE QUESTIONS
Scope Management

	3rd Time	2nd Time	1st Time

1) A WBS numbering system should allow project staff to:
   A. Estimate costs of WBS elements
   B. Provide project justification
   C. Identify the level at which individual WBS elements are found
   D. Use it in project management software

2) A chief characteristic of the Delphi technique is:
   A. Extrapolation from historical records
   B. Intuitive expert opinion
   C. Analytical hierarchy process
   D. A guess

3) The work breakdown structure can be an effective aid for _____ communications.
   A. Team
   B. Company
   C. Customer
   D. A, B, and C

4) A key attribute of scope verification is:
   A. Improved cost estimates
   B. Customer acceptance of project efforts
   C. Improved schedule estimates
   D. An improved project management information system

5) _____ contains detailed descriptions of work packages.
   A. WBS Dictionaries
   B. Scope of work
   C. Budget estimates
   D. Cost estimates

6) In what phase of the life cycle is the project scope determined?
   A. Initiation
   B. Planning
   C. Execution
   D. None of the above

7) A project charter includes:
   A. Precedence diagramming methods
   B. Task estimates
   C. Detailed resource estimates
   D. The business' need for the project

8) As the project becomes more complex, the level of uncertainty in the scope:
   A. Remains the same
   B. Decreases
   C. Decreases then increases
   D. Increases

9) Project plans are developed by the:
   A. Senior manager
   B. Functional managers
   C. Project manager
   D. Project team

10) The WBS can be used for which of the following:
   A. Communicating with the customer
   B. Showing calendar dates for each task
   C. Showing the functional managers for each team member
   D. Showing the business need for the project

11) During a project team meeting a team member suggests an enhancement to the scope of work that is beyond the scope of the project charter. The project manager points out that the team needs to concentrate on completing all the work and only the work required. This is an example of:
   A. Domineering behavior
   B. Scope management
   C. Project charter
   D. Scope decomposition

12) Scope verification should be done:
   A. At the end of the project
   B. At the beginning of the project
   C. During each phase of the project
   D. Once during planning

13) Management by Objectives works only if:
   A. It is supported by management
   B. The rules are written down
   C. The project does not impact the objectives
   D. The project includes the objectives in the charter

14) The customer wants to make a major change to the scope of work when the project is mostly complete. The project manager should:
   A. Make the change
   B. Inform the customer of the impact of the change
   C. Refuse the change
   D. Complain to management

© May 2000 (Registered) Rita Mulcahy, PMP at RMC – Project Management
PHONE: (612) 929-7539, EMAIL: rita@rmcproject.com, WEB: rmcproject.com

15) A key reason to use a work breakdown structure is to:
    A. Organize the work
    B. Prevent work from slipping through the cracks
    C. Provide a basis for estimating the project
    D. All of the above

16) The process of creating a work breakdown structure results in:
    A. A project schedule
    B. Team buy-in
    C. A project completion date
    D. A list of risks

17) In order to manage a project effectively work should be broken down into small pieces. Which of the following does not describe how far each task should be broken down?
    A. Can be completed in under 80 hours
    B. Cannot be logically subdivided further
    C. Is done by one person
    D. Can be realistically estimated

18) A project manager finds out what their company's objectives are and how the project fits into them. This is an example of taking into account _____.
    A. Responsibility charts
    B. Management by objectives
    C. The project's future
    D. The work breakdown structure

19) What does having a project charter do for the project managers?
    A. Describes the details of what needs to be done
    B. Describes the names of all team members
    C. Gives the project manager authority
    D. Describes the project's history

20) A project manager may use _____ to make sure the team clearly knows what work is included in each of their tasks.
    A. A project scope of work
    B. A project charter
    C. A WBS dictionary
    D. A risk management plan

21) Linear programming is an example of what type of project selection criteria?
    A. Constrained optimization
    B. Comparative approach
    C. Benefit measurement
    D. Impact analysis

ANSWERS:
1 C
2 B
3 D
4 B
5 A
6 B
7 D
8 D
9 D
10 A
11 B
12 C
13 A
14 B
15 D
16 B
17 C
18 B
19 C
20 C
21 A

Chapter 5

Time Management
(PMBOK® Chapter 6)

The questions on time management tend to be some of the hardest. First, the exam asks questions about network diagrams that are no longer in current practice. Second, most people are not familiar with the techniques for dealing with unrealistic schedules (crashing and fast tracking). To explain the trouble areas and make this chapter easier, I have decided to describe the time management items in the order of their occurrence on a real project instead of in their order in the HOT TOPICS section.

HOT TOPICS in order of importance:
- Network Diagrams
  - Dependencies
    - Mandatory
    - Discretionary
    - External
  - Methods to draw
    - Activity-on-arrow (ADM)
    - Activity-on-node (PDM)
- Critical Path
- Slack (float)
- Lag
- Estimating methods
  - PERT
  - CPM
  - Monte Carlo simulation
- Resource leveling
- Shortening the schedule
  - Crashing
  - Fast tracking
- Scheduling tools
  - Network Diagrams
  - Bar (Gantt) charts
  - Milestone charts
  - Flow Charts
- Heuristics
- See the **PMBOK** for:
  - GERT (page 63)

In order to answer all time management questions correctly, you need a thorough understanding of network diagrams and scheduling methods. You should have an understanding of the manual calculations of network diagrams. You do not have to know project management software (which is really only a scheduling tool)!

Be careful reading this chapter. It contains many terms that are incorrect but commonly used. Make sure that you understand how they are presented here.

NETWORK DIAGRAM or Logic Diagram (page 64): The network diagram shows HOW the project tasks will flow from beginning to end. Once estimates are available for each task, it also proves how long the project will take to complete. A network diagram is created after the project charter, project staffing, and WBS.

A network diagram is created by taking the project tasks (or work packages) from the lowest level of the WBS and putting them in their order of completion from project beginning to end. This is called activity sequencing. The resulting diagram may look like this:

Did You Know
The general name for this is a Network Diagram NOT a PERT chart!

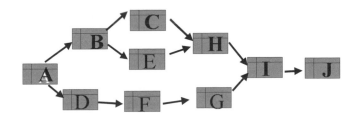

TYPES OF DEPENDENCIES – The sequence of tasks depends on the following dependencies:
- **MANDATORY DEPENDENCY (HARD LOGIC)** – Inherent in the nature of the work being done (e.g., you must design before you can construct).

- **DISCRETIONARY DEPENDENCY (PREFERRED, PREFERENTIAL, OR SOFT LOGIC)** – Based on experience, desire, or references.

- **EXTERNAL DEPENDENCY** – Based on the needs or desires of a party outside the project (e.g., government or suppliers).

METHODS TO DRAW – There are two ways to draw a network diagram, activity-on-arrow or activity-on-node. (NOTE: Activity-on-arrow is sometimes called activity-on-line.) At one time there may have been a reason to draw them one way or the other, but with today's software, the method no longer matters. You should, however, know both methods for the exam. Memorize the following and then forget it after the exam in favor of how your project management software handles network diagrams.

ACTIVITY-ON-NODE (AON) OR PRECEDENCE DIAGRAMMING METHOD (PDM) – In this method, nodes (or boxes) are used to represent tasks. Arrows show task dependencies. This method adds lag relationships (described later) to PERT or CPM and is illustrated in the diagram on the previous page and uses:
- There can be four types of relationships between tasks:

  Finish-to-start – a task must finish before the next can start

  Finish-to-finish – a task must finish before the next may finish

  Start-to-start – a task must start before the next can start

  Start-to-finish – a task must start before the next may finish

- But does not use dummies (described below).

ACTIVITY-ON-ARROW (AOA) OR ARROW DIAGRAMMING METHOD (ADM) – In this method, illustrated below, the arrows are used to represent tasks. This method uses:
- Only finish-to-start relationships between tasks

- May use dummy activities. Dummies are usually represented by a dotted line and are inserted simply to show dependencies between tasks. They do not require work or take time. See the picture below.

- According to the exam, PERT and CPM estimating techniques (described on the next page) can only be drawn on an AOA diagram.

An Activity on Arrow
Network Diagram
(with Task F as a dummy)

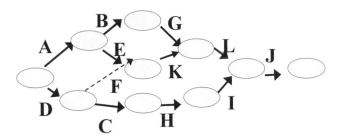

ESTIMATING METHODS (page 67): Three main methods are used for estimating the duration of a project. Please see the Cost Chapter for further estimating topics.

- CPM
- PERT
- Monte Carlo

CPM (Critical Path Method) NOTE: Although this technique may use the words "critical path," it does not refer to finding the "critical path." It refers to estimating based on one time estimate per activity!

- One time estimate per task
- Emphasis on controlling cost and leaving the schedule flexible
- Drawn only on an activity-on-arrow (AOA) diagram
- Can have dummies

ESTIMATING USING CPM – When estimating using a one-time estimate (CPM), one estimate per task is received. For example, the person doing the estimating in effect says that the task will take exactly five weeks. This method uses only a most likely time estimate.

© May 2000 (Registered) Rita Mulcahy, PMP at RMC – Project Management

PHONE: (612) 929-7539, EMAIL: rita@rmcproject.com, WEB: rmcproject.com

It is illegal to copy, transmit, or reproduce any part of this document without specific written approval from the author!

55

PERT (Program evaluation and review technique):
- Three time estimates per activity
    - Optimistic
    - Pessimistic
    - Most likely
- Emphasis on meeting schedules with flexibility on costs
- Drawn only on an activity-on-arrow (AOA) diagram
- Can have dummies

ESTIMATING USING PERT – PERT is superior to CPM because it requires three time estimates per task and uses the distribution's mean instead of the most likely time estimate in CPM. In this form of estimating, the individual estimating the task provides an optimistic, pessimistic, and most likely estimate for each task. You must know three formulas:

PERT formula: $(P+4M+O)/6$	Standard deviation of a task using PERT: $(P-O)/6$	Variance of a task using PERT: $\left[\dfrac{P-O}{6}\right]^2$

Exercise – PERT:

INSTRUCTIONS: Test yourself! Complete the chart using the formulas above. All estimates are in hours.

TASK	O	M	P	PERT DURATIONS	TASK STANDARD DEVIATION	TASK VARIANCE
A	14	27	47			
B	41	60	89			
C	39	44	48			
D	29	37	42			

Answer: It is good practice for the exam to work with three digits. Only round to two digits when you are done answering a specific question on the exam. Remember that square is not times two but a number times itself.

TASK	O	M	P	PERT	TASK STANDARD DEVIATION	TASK VARIANCE
A	14	27	47	28.166	5.5	30.25
B	41	60	89	61.666	8	64
C	39	44	48	43.833	1.5	2.25
D	29	37	42	36.5	2.166	4.693

These simple calculations are all you need to know for PERT. See also PMBOK® page 116.

Exercise – PERT, part 2:

INSTRUCTIONS: Assuming that the tasks listed above make up the entire critical path for the project, how long will the project take?

Answer: 170.165 hours +/- 10.059 hours at one standard deviation. 170.165 is found by adding the PERT estimates for each of the critical path tasks (in this case all the tasks listed.) The +/- 10.059 represents the standard deviation of the estimate (the range of the estimate) and is found by adding the variances of the critical path tasks and taking the square root. (Statistically, the rule is that you cannot add standard deviations but must add the variances and take the square root.) In this case the project would not take 170.165 hours but between 180.224 hours and 160.106 hours.

MONTE CARLO SIMULATION (page 118 and 66 under simulation): This method of estimating uses a computer to simulate the outcome of a project based on PERT estimates (optimistic, pessimistic, and most likely estimates) and the network diagram, but does not use the PERT formula. The simulation can tell you:

- The probability of completing the project on any specific day
- The probability of completing the project for any specific amount of cost
- The probability of any task actually being on the critical path
- The overall project risk.

See the chart on page 118 of the PMBOK®. PMI® suggests that **Monte Carlo simulation will create a project duration that is closer to reality than CPM or PERT.**

OTHER ESTIMATING NOTES – You should know that people doing the work (not the project manager or senior managers) should create estimates. The role of the project manager is to:
- Provide the team with enough information to properly estimate each task
- Complete a sanity check of the estimate
- Formulate a reserve (more on this later)

Estimates can come from any of the following:
- Guess. (Yes, this is okay. Remember we are estimating based on a WBS. Estimating a small task by guessing will be more accurate than doing the same for a larger task.)
- Historical records (This is a PMI®-ism, see chapter 1)
- Actual costs – Labor, material, overhead, risk
- Benchmarks – Comparing your performance to another company's.
- CPM
- PERT

CRITICAL PATH: Once you create a network diagram and estimate tasks, you can find the critical path.

Exercise:

INSTRUCTIONS: Test yourself! What is a critical path and how does it help the project manager?

Answer: The critical path is the longest path through a network diagram and determines the earliest completion of the project. Although the critical path may change over time, it helps prove how long the project will take and indicates to the project manager which tasks need more monitoring. The critical path almost always has no slack (defined later.)

Many critical path-related questions show up on the exam regarding juggling between time, cost, risk, and quality to keep the critical path an acceptable length. See crashing and fast tracking described later.

Please note that although CPM does stand for "Critical Path Method," a critical path can be found using CPM, Pert, or Monte Carlo!

Exercise:

Task	Preceding activity	Estimate in months
START		0
D	START	4
A	START	6
F	D, A	7
E	D	8
G	F, E	5
B	F	5
H	G	7
C	H	8
END	C, B	0

Answer: The critical path (project duration) is 33 months.

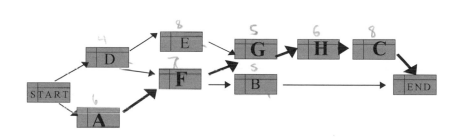

SLACK (FLOAT): The amount of time a task can be delayed without delaying the project. Tasks on the critical path almost always have no slack. Slack is found by finding the difference between the early start and late start of a task. The output from most project management software will supply a list of the slack for each task. Such information helps team members juggle multiple projects by telling them how much time flexibility they have on each task they are working on.

Slack is sometimes broken down into:
- Free Slack (float) – the amount of time a task can be delayed without delaying the early start date of its successor, and
- Total Slack (float) – The amount of time a task can be delayed without delaying the project completion date.

LAG: Inserted waiting time between tasks. For example, you must wait three days after pouring concrete before you can install the frame for a house.

Exercise: Try it! Find the slack of tasks B, D, and E from the picture above.

Answer: The answers are 15 months, 1 month and 1 month respectively.

Exercise:

INSTRUCTIONS: You can expect around seven questions on network diagrams on the exam so a little more practice is in order. Here is an example of a form of question that has a paragraph of information and four questions that relate to it. You may see four questions of this type on the exam for a total of sixteen questions but they will not all be about network diagrams.

TASK	ESTIMATE In weeks	
START- A	3	
START- B	9	
A-C	3	
B-C	dummy	
B-E	2	
C-D	2	
C-E	1	
E-END	4	
D-END	2	

1. What is the critical path? _____

2. If the duration of activity C-E changes to 2, what is the effect on the project? _____

3. What task(s) must be completed before task C-D begins? _____

4. If management tells you to complete the project two weeks early, what is the project float? Does the critical path change? _____

Answer: The critical path (project duration) is 15 weeks.

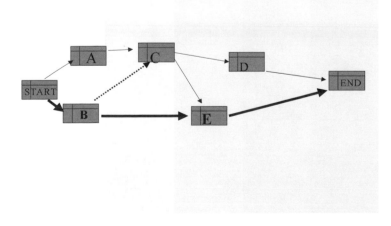

Answer: Continued:

1. The critical path is Start-B, B-E, and E-End.
2. If C-E changes from 1 to 2, the critical path would be:
   - Start-B, B-E, E-End, as well as
   - Start-B, B-C, C-E, E-End
3. The tasks that must be completed before C-D begins are Start-A, A-C, and Start-B.
4. The project float would be minus 2, and the critical path would not change.

These are good questions because they test your knowledge about such questions as:

- Can there be more than one critical path? Yes.

- Do you want there to be? No, it increases risk.

- Can a critical path run over a dummy? Yes.

- Why is a dummy included in a network diagram? To show interdependencies of tasks.

- Can a critical path change? Yes.

- Can there be negative float? Yes, it shows you are behind.

- Does the network diagram change when the end date changes? No, but the project manager should investigate options such as fast tracking and crashing the schedule to meet the new date and then change the network diagram accordingly.

- Would you leave the project with a negative float? No, you would crash or fast track.

RESOURCE LEVELING (page 68): Resource leveling is a little-used tool in project management software that allows you to level the peaks and valleys of resource use from one month to another. It allows you to have a more stable number of resources used on your project but lets schedule and cost slip in favor of leveling resources.

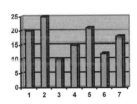

HEURISTICS (page 68): A heuristic, no matter how it is used, means rule of thumb. (This is the only question I got wrong on the exam! Okay, I just wanted to see if you were really reading this.) Several types of heuristics exist: some are scheduling, estimating, planning, and resource leveling. One such heuristic is the 80-20 rule which, in quality, suggests that 80% of quality problems are caused by 20% of potential sources of problems.

SCHEDULING TOOLS AND THEIR BENEFITS (page 69-70): Once a network diagram and estimates are completed, it is time to put the information into a schedule. The difference between a time estimate and a schedule is that the schedule is calendar-based.

Three main ways to show a schedule are bar chart (Gantt chart), network diagram, and milestone chart. (Please see the illustrations in PMBOK® pages 69-70.) You must be able to answer questions about when to use each.

Exercise – Scheduling Tools:

<u>INSTRUCTIONS</u>: Test yourself! Fill in the answers to the following questions in the spaces provided below.

Under what circumstances would you want to use a network diagram instead of a Gantt chart?	
Under what circumstances would you want to use a milestone chart instead of a Gantt chart?	
Under what circumstances would you want to use a Gantt chart instead of a network diagram?	

Answer:

Under what circumstances would you use a network diagram instead of a Gantt chart? (**NOTE**: Some project management software packages make an attempt to draw lines between tasks on a Gantt chart to show interdependencies. The result is so confusing as to be useless. Ignore this aspect of software when answering these type of questions.)	To show interdependencies between tasks.
Under what circumstances would you want to use a milestone chart instead of a Gantt chart?	To report to senior management.
Under what circumstances would you want to use a Gantt chart instead of a network diagram?	To track progress. To report to the team.

A few more comments on the different scheduling tools. For examples of these tools, see PMBOK® pages 69-70.

BAR (GANTT) CHARTS
- Weak planning tool but effective progress reporting and control tool
- Does not show interdependencies of tasks
- Does not help organize the project more effectively

NETWORK DIAGRAM (PERT, CPM, PDM)
- Shows interdependencies of tasks and work flow
- Aids in effectively planning and organizing the work
- Provides a basis for project control

MILESTONE CHARTS (MILESTONES HAVE NO DURATION!)
- Similar to bar charts but only shows major events
- A good tool for reporting to management and the customer

FLOW CHARTS
- Depicts workflow and is not commonly used for project management

SHORTENING THE SCHEDULE (page 68 under duration compression): One of the most common problems projects have is an unrealistic time frame. Most project managers have problems with unrealistic time frames and are not aware of how to deal with them.

Crashing and fast tracking are two ways to shorten the project schedule. This most often needs to happen under two circumstances. First, management says the project duration is too long. Second, a change has been made to the project.

Many project managers handle these situations by going back to the team and saying, "cut 20% off your estimates." This is an inappropriate project management technique so you can expect to see it listed on the exam as a possible choice. The reason it is inappropriate is that more effective choices exist. Why shorten every task? To shorten the project schedule, look at the critical path tasks and crash or fast track those tasks.

CRASHING: Adding more resources to the critical path. This can take the form of moving resources from non-critical tasks or adding extra resources to the task. Crashing almost always results in increased costs.

For example, using the following diagram, resources could be added to task G or any other task on the critical path (assuming that such a proposition was logical based on the nature of the work). These resources could be acquired from task B or any task not on the critical path, or from outside the project.

Network Diagram Example

FAST TRACKING: Doing more tasks in parallel. Note that fast tracking often results in rework and usually increases risk.

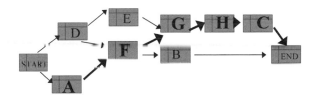

For example, what task would you fast track to shorten the project length in the picture on the right? Task H (or any other task on the critical path assuming it is logical due to the nature of the work) could be fast tracked by making it occur at the same time, or in parallel with Task G. Or Task C could be fast tracked by having part of it done concurrently with Task H.

In crashing or fast tracking, it is best to see all potential choices and then select the choice or choices that have the least impact on the project.

© May 2000 (Registered) Rita Mulcahy, PMP at RMC – Project Management
PHONE: (612) 929-7539, EMAIL: rita@rmcproject.com, WEB: rmcproject.com

Exercise:

INSTRUCTIONS: Test yourself on crashing and fast tracking! What option presented below would you select to save three months on the project assuming that the tasks listed below represent the critical path?

Task	Original Duration in Months	Crash Duration in Months	Time Savings	Original Cost in dollars	Crash Cost	Extra Cost	Cost Per Month	Risk Impact
F	14	12	2	10,000	14,000	4,000	2,000	HIGH
A	9	7	2	17,000	27,000	10,000	5,000	LOW
H	3	2	1	25,000	26,000	1,000	1,000	LOW
G	7	6	1	14,000	16,000	2,000	2,000	HIGH
C	11	8	3	27,000	36,000	9,000	3,000	NONE

Answer: There is no answer! The answer would depend on whether cost or risk is more important on the project.

Exercise:

Lets assume that time is of most importance followed by cost, such questions are on the exam. What would be your answer?

Answer: The answer would be to select tasks F and H for an additional cost of $5,000. If risk were second to time in importance the answer would be to select task C for an additional cost of $9,000. The exam will probably not include a risk column because risk (nor quality) is not considered when most people crash or fast track their projects. Without a risk column simply pick the least cost alternative.

SAMPLE QUESTIONS

Time Management

	3rd Time	2nd Time	1st Time

1) The _____ is a technique used to predict project duration by analyzing which sequence of activities has the least amount of scheduling flexibility.
- A. Critical path technique
- B. Flow chart technique
- C. Precedence diagramming method
- D. Work breakdown structure

2) A dependency that requires that design be completed before manufacturing can start is an example of:
- A. Discretionary dependency
- B. External dependency
- C. Mandatory dependency
- D. Scope dependency

3) Bar charts generally illustrate ___ better than network diagrams.
- A. Logical relationships
- B. Critical paths
- C. Resource trade-off
- D. Progress or status

4) The estimate for Task A is O – 3, P – 7, M – 4. What is the standard deviation for Task A?
- A. 5/6 of a day
- B. 2/3 of a day
- C. 1 ½ days
- D. 4 days

5) A heuristic is a:
- A. Control tool
- B. Scheduling method
- C. Planning tools
- D. Rule of thumb

6) Lag means:
- A. Amount of time a task can be delayed without delaying the project
- B. Amount of time a task can be delayed without delaying the early start date of its successor
- C. Waiting time
- D. Calculated by making a forward and backward pass

7) A critical path is shown on what project management tool:
   A. WBS
   B. Network Diagram
   C. Project Control Plan
   D. Project Charter

8) Dummy activities are not used on which type of network diagram:
   A. CPM
   B. Detailed
   C. PDM
   D. PERT

9) The project manager has asked a few of the team members for assistance in structuring the project milestones. The team has never worked on a project before and needs instructions about milestones. The project manager should tell the team that milestones have:
   A. An unlimited duration
   B. A duration less than the activity it represents
   C. No duration
   D. A duration greater than the activity it represents

10) A project manager is in the middle of the execution phase on a very large construction project when he discovers that the time needed to complete the project is longer than the time available. What should he do?
   A. Contact the customer and tell them that their required date cannot be met
   B. Meet with management and tell them that their required date cannot be met
   C. Crash or fast track the project
   D. Crash or fast track the project and go to management with options

11) During planning you sit down and estimate the time needed for each task and total them to determine the project estimate. This duration is what you commit to completing the project. What is wrong in this scenario?
   A. The team did not create the estimate and estimating takes too long using that method
   B. The team did not create the estimate and a network diagram was not used
   C. The estimate is too long and should be created by management
   D. The project estimate should be the same as the customer's required completion date

12) If the optimistic estimate for a task is 12 days, pessimistic is 18 days, what is the most likely estimate?
   A. 15 days
   B. 13 days
   C. 16 days
   D. Not enough information

13) If the optimistic estimate for a task is 12 days, pessimistic is 18 days, what is the standard deviation of the task?
    A. 1
    B. 1.3
    C. 6
    D. 3

14) What does the standard deviation have to do with risk?
    A. Nothing
    B. Standard deviation tells you if the estimate is accurate
    C. Standard deviation tells you how unsure the estimate is
    D. Standard deviation tells you if the estimate includes a pad

15) Monte Carlo analysis gives you:
    A. An indication of the risk involved in the project
    B. A way to estimate a task's length
    C. A way to simulate the order in which tasks occur
    D. A way to prove to management that extra staff is needed

16) Task slack is determined by:
    A. Performing a Monte Carlo analysis
    B. Determining the waiting time between tasks
    C. Determining lag
    D. The amount of time the task can be delayed before it delays the critical path

17) A project has three critical paths. What difference does this make to the project?
    A. It makes it easier to manage
    B. It increases the project risk
    C. It requires more people
    D. The situation is not possible

18) If project time and cost are not as important as the number of resources used each month, you might:
    A. Perform a Monte Carlo analysis
    B. Fast track the project
    C. Perform resource leveling
    D. Analyze the life cycle costs

19) Under what circumstances would you use a milestone chart instead of a Gantt chart?
    A. For project planning
    B. For reporting to stakeholders
    C. For reporting to management
    D. For risk analysis

20) Your project plan results in a project schedule that is too long. If the project network diagram cannot change but you have extra personnel resources, you would:
   A. Fast track the project
   B. Perform a Monte Carlo analysis
   C. Crash the project
   D. Perform a value analysis

21) An activity-on-node diagram is different from an activity-on-arrow diagram in that it:
   A. Is drawn with dark lines
   B. Has four relationships between tasks
   C. Has only finish to finish relationships
   D. May use dummy activities

22) You have decided to estimate your project using one time estimate per activity or task. You would then be using which method?
   A. PERT
   B. PDM
   C. CPM
   D. WBS

23) In creating your network diagram, you determine that waiting time is needed between two tasks. Another name for waiting time is:
   A. Slack
   B. Float
   C. Lag
   D. CPM

24) Your customer notifies you that the project must be completed two days earlier. What do you do?
   A. Tell them that the project's critical path does not allow the project to be finished earlier
   B. Tell your boss
   C. Meet with the team and look for options for crashing or fast tracking the critical path
   D. Work hard and see what the project status is next month

25) In trying to get the project completed faster, the project manager looks at the cost associated with crashing each task. A more complete approach to crashing would be to also look at ____:
   A. The risk impact of crashing each task
   B. The customer's opinion of what tasks to crash
   C. The day of the week the task is to take place
   D. The project phase in which the task is due to occur

26) A project manager is trying to coordinate all the tasks on the project and has determined the following. What is the critical path for this project?

Task 1 can start immediately and has an estimated duration of 1 week. Task 2 can start after task 1 is completed and has an estimated duration of 4 weeks. Task 3 can start after task 2 is completed and has an estimated duration of 5 weeks. Task 4 can start after task 1 is completed and must be completed when task 3 is completed. Its estimated duration is 8 weeks.
   A.   10
   B.   11
   C.   14
   D.   8

27) Based on the data in the question above, if task 4 takes 10 weeks, what is the critical path?
   A.   10
   B.   11
   C.   14
   D.   8

ANSWERS:
1 A
2 C
3 D
4 B
5 D
6 C
7 B
8 C
9 C
10 D
11 B
12 D
13 A
14 C
15 A
16 D
17 B
18 C
19 C
20 C
21 B
22 C
23 C
24 C
25 A
26 A
27 B

Chapter 6

Cost Management

(PMBOK® Chapter 7)

The questions on cost management are not difficult. Many people are nervous about questions relating to earned value. To ease your mind I will tell you that no more than five questions on earned value have been on the exam for the last four years. To make it even easier, for the last four years only four or five questions on the exam have required a calculation.

Cost includes many topics that have only one question. Therefore, most of the topics listed below under accounting standards should be mentioned only ONCE on the test. Remember, you do not have to be an accountant to pass this exam. With a little study, the questions on cost should be easy.

HOT TOPICS in order of importance:

- Inputs to estimating
- Cost Estimating
  - Analogous
  - Bottom up
  - Parametric
- Earned value analysis
- Progress reporting (50/50, 20/80, 0/100)
- Accuracy of estimates
  - Order of magnitude
  - Budget
  - Definitive
- Cost risk
- Accounting standards
  - Present value
  - Net present value
  - Internal rate of return
  - Variable/fixed costs
  - Direct/indirect costs
  - Benefit cost ratio
  - Payback period
  - Opportunity cost
  - Sunk cost
  - Law of diminishing returns
  - Depreciation
    - Straight line
    - Accelerated
  - Life cycle costing
  - Value analysis
  - Working capital

Many time topics relate to cost and have been covered in Chapter 5, Time Management. As you read the PMBOK®, you will see such recurring themes as:

- Estimating should be based on a WBS to improve accuracy.

- Estimating should be done by the person doing the work.

- Having historical records is a key element in improving estimates.

- Costs (schedule, scope, resources) should be managed to estimates.

- A cost (schedule, scope, resource) baseline should be kept and not changed.

- Plans should be revised, as necessary, during completion of the work.

- Corrective action should be taken when cost problems (schedule, scope, and resource) occur.

INPUTS TO ESTIMATING (or what do you need before you estimate costs or time): In order to create a good estimate, you need the following before you begin estimating:

- WBS

- Network diagram – Costs cannot be estimated until it is known how the project will flow from beginning to end.

- Schedule – For multi-year projects, the cost of a task is usually different if it is completed in one year compared to another.

- Historical records

- Resource pool – An understanding of the available resources or the resources assigned.

- Risks

COST ESTIMATING TECHNIQUES:

ANALOGOUS ESTIMATING (page 66) or Top Down – Top or middle managers use expert judgement or the actual time and cost of a previous, similar project as the basis for estimating the current project. The project manager must then allocate this estimate of time and cost to all the project work that needs to be done. Analogous estimating is a form of expert judgement.

BOTTOM UP ESTIMATING – With this technique, the people doing the work create cost and schedule estimates. Estimates, based on the WBS, are rolled up to get a project total.

PARAMETRIC ESTIMATING – Uses project characteristics in a mathematical model to predict project costs. For example, cost per line-of-code or cost per lane mile. You should also know the two types of parametric estimates:
- Regression analysis (you do not need to know what it is)
- Learning curve – The 500th room you paint will cost less than the first because you learn as you work.

COMPUTERIZED ESTIMATING TOOLS – These are commercially available packages that will help estimate projects in many industries.

Exercise:

INSTRUCTIONS: Answer the questions below and put your answers in the spaces provided.

What Are The Advantages Of Analogous Estimating?	What Are The Disadvantages?

What Are The Advantages Of Bottom-Up Estimating?	What Are The Disadvantages?

Answer: There are many possible answers. The purpose is to get you thinking about the differences so that you can answer any questions on the topic, no matter how they may be worded.

Advantages Of Analogous Estimating	Disadvantages
Quick	Less accurate
Tasks need not be identified	Estimates prepared with a limited amount of detailed information and understanding of the project
Less costly to create	Requires considerable experience to do well
Gives the project manager an idea of the level of management's expectations	Infighting at the highest management levels to gain the biggest piece of the pie without knowing what the pie is
Overall project costs will be capped	Extremely difficult for projects with uncertainty
Advantages Of Bottom-Up Estimating	**Disadvantages**
More accurate	Takes time and expense to do this form of estimating
Gains buy-in from the team	Tendency for the team to pad estimates
Based on a detailed analysis of the project	Requires that the project be defined and understood
Provides a basis for monitoring and control	Team infighting to gain the biggest piece of the pie

PROGRESS REPORTING: A progress report is a useful method to control costs. Many project managers determine how much work has been accomplished by asking team members for an estimate of *percent complete* for each task. On projects where work cannot be measured, this estimate is simply a guess. This is time consuming and almost always a complete waste of time because a guess does not provide a confident estimate of the actual percent complete.

If a project has been planned using a WBS, and tasks require about 80 hours of work, than we have alternatives to percent complete. Because tasks will be completed faster and more frequently, we can forget percent complete and use one of the following:

50/50 RULE – A task is considered 50% complete when it begins and gets credit for the last 50% only when it is completed.

20/80 RULE – A task is considered 20% complete when it begins and gets credit for the last 80% only when it is completed.

0/100 RULE – A task does not get credit for partial completion, only full completion.

COST RISK: Sometimes a question on the exam will cross boundaries between risk, procurement, and cost. Cost risk is best explained with an example question: "Who has the cost risk in a fixed price contract, the buyer or seller?" The answer is seller.

EARNED VALUE ANALYSIS (page 108): Earned value analysis is a method of performance measurement. Many project managers manage their project's performance by comparing planned to actual results. A major problem with this method is that it looks at time and cost separately. You could easily be on time but overspend according to your plan. A better method is earned value because it integrates cost, schedule, and scope.

Two things about earned value you must know for the exam: the formulas and interpretation. As time goes on, I expect interpretation will be more important than memorizing the formulas.

TERMS TO KNOW:

TERM	DESCRIPTION	INTERPRETATION
BCWS	Budgeted Cost of Work Scheduled	How much work SHOULD be done?
BCWP	Budgeted Cost of Work Performed or "Earned Value"	How much work IS done on a budgeted basis or how much did we budget for the work we did?
ACWP	Actual Cost of Work Performed	How much did the IS DONE work cost, or how much did we spend to date?
BAC	Budget at Completion	How much did you BUDGET for the TOTAL JOB?
EAC	Estimate at Completion	What do we currently expect the TOTAL project to cost?
ETC	Estimate to Complete	From this point on, how much MORE do we expect it to cost to finish the job?
VAC	Variance at Completion	How much over or under budget do we expect to be?

FORMULAS AND INTERPRETATION TO MEMORIZE:

NAME	FORMULA	INTERPRETATION
VARIANCE	Plan – Actual	
COST VARIANCE (CV)	BCWP – ACWP	NEGATIVE is over budget, POSITIVE is under budget
SCHEDULE VARIANCE (SV)	BCWP – BCWS	NEGATIVE is behind schedule, POSITIVE is ahead of schedule
COST PERFORMANCE INDEX (CPI)	$\frac{BCWP}{ACWP}$	I am [only] getting _____ cents out of every $1.
SCHEDULE PERFORMANCE INDEX (SPI)	$\frac{BCWP}{BCWS}$	I am [only] progressing at _____% of the rate originally planned.
ESTIMATE AT COMPLETION (EAC)	$\frac{BAC}{CPI}$	As of now we expect the total project to cost $ _____.
ESTIMATE TO COMPLETE (ETC)	EAC - ACWP	How much will it cost from now to the completion of the project?
VARIANCE AT COMPLETION (VAC)	BAC - EAC	When the project is completed, how much more or less will we have spent?

NOTE: There are many ways to calculate EAC. The formula above is the one most often asked on the exam.

TRICKS FOR QUESTIONS ABOUT EARNED VALUE: These tricks work! Make sure you know them.

1. Notice that BCWP comes first in every formula. Remembering this one fact alone should help you get about half the earned value questions right. (Aren't you glad you purchased this book?)
2. If it is a variance, the formula is BCWP minus something.
3. If it is an index, it is BCWP divided by something.
4. If the formula relates to cost, use ACWP.
5. If the formula relates to schedule, use BCWS.
6. For interpretation: negative is bad and positive is good. Thus a –200 cost variance means that you are behind (over) budget.
7. One of the earned value questions people answer incorrectly requires that you differentiate between EAC and ETC. Try this exercise. Which line represents ETC?

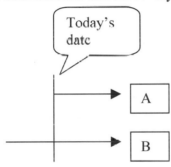

The answer is A.

Many people preparing to take the PMP® exam are worried about earned value. You should be aware that only four questions on earned value have been on the exam for the last four years. Not all of the earned value questions require calculations. (Please see the sample questions at the end of the chapter.) See also PMBOK® pages 81, 108 and 109.

Exercise – Earned Value: The best way to learn this technique is to do it. I have designed these exercises to give you a chance to practice calculations AND interpretation. Keep in mind that these exercises are HARDER than the questions on the exam. If you get them right, you should not have to study earned value any more. GOOD LUCK!!!

The Fence #1
Earned Value Exercise #1

*You have a project to build a new fence.
The fence is four sided as shown:*

Each side is to take one day and is budgeted for US $1,000 per side. The sides are planned to be completed one after the other. Today is the end of day three.

INSTRUCTIONS: Using the project status chart below, calculate BCWS, BCWP, etc. When completed, check your answers on the answer sheet on the following page. Interpretation on the exam is also important. Can you interpret what each answer means?

TASK	DAY1	DAY2	DAY3	DAY4	STATUS AT THE END OF DAY 3
Side 1	S----------F				Complete, spent US $1,000
Side 2		S------------PF	----F		Complete, spent US $1,200
Side 3			PS----S-----PF		Half done, spent US $600
Side 4				PS ---------PF	Not yet started

KEY: S - Start, F - Finish, PS - Planned Start, and PF - Planned Finish

WHAT IS:	CALCULATION	ANSWER	INTERPRETATION OF THE ANSWER
BCWS			
BCWP			
ACWP			
BAC			
CV			
CPI			
SV			
SPI			
EAC			
ETC			
VAC			

Answer Earned Value Exercise - The Fence #1

WHAT IS:	CALCULATION	ANSWER	INTERPRETATION OF THE ANSWER
BCWS	1,000 plus 1,000 plus 1,000	3,000	We should have done $3,000 worth of work.
BCWP	Complete, complete, half done or 1,000 plus 1,000 plus 500	2,500	We budgeted $2,500 for the work we completed.
ACWP	1,000 plus 1,200 plus 600	2,800	We actually spent $2,800.
BAC	1,000 plus 1,000 plus 1,000 plus 1,000	4,000	Our project budget is $4,000.
CV	2,500 minus 2,800	-300	We are over budget by $300.
CPI	2,500 divided by 2,800	.893	We are only getting 89 cents out of every dollar we put into the project.
SV	2,500 minus 3,000	-500	We are behind schedule.
SPI	2,500 divided by 3,000	.833	We are only progressing at 83% of the rate planned.
EAC	4,000 divided by .893	4,479	We currently estimate that the total project will cost $4,479.
ETC	4,479 minus 2,800	1,679	We need to spend $1,679 to finish the project.
VAC	4,000 minus 4479	-479	We currently expect to be $479 over budget when the project is completed.

NOTE: If your answers differ check your rounding. It is best to round to three decimal points.

The Fence #2
Earned Value Exercise #2

You have a project to build a new fence.
The fence is four sided as shown:

Each side is to take one day and is budgeted for US $1,000 per side. **IN THIS CASE, ASSUME THAT THE SIDES HAVE A FINISH TO FINISH RELATIONSHIP INSTEAD OF A FINISH TO START RELATIONSHIP!** *Today is the end of day three.*

INSTRUCTIONS: Using the project status chart below, fill in the blanks in the chart and check your answers on the answer sheet on the following page.

TASK	DAY1	DAY2	DAY3	DAY4	STATUS AT THE END OF DAY 3
Side 1	S----------F				Complete, spent US $1,000
Side 2		S-----F-----PF			Complete, spent US $900
Side 3		S----	PS---------PF		50% done, spent US $1000
Side 4			S----	PS --------PF	75% done, spent US $300

KEY: S - Start, F -Finish, PS - Planned Start, PF - Planned Finish

WHAT IS:	CALCULATION	ANSWER	INTERPRETATION OF THE ANSWER
BCWS			
BCWP			
ACWP			
BAC			
CV			
CPI			
SV			
SPI			
EAC			
ETC			
VAC			

Answer Earned Value Exercise - The Fence #2

WHAT IS:	CALCULATION	ANSWER	INTERPRETATION OF THE ANSWER
BCWS	1,000 plus 1,000 plus 1,000	3,000	We should have done $3,000 worth of work.
BCWP	Complete, complete, half done, 75% done or 1,000 plus 1,000 plus 500, plus 750	3,250	We budgeted $3,250 for the work we completed.
ACWP	1,000 plus 900, plus 1,000, plus 300	3,200	We actually spent $3,200.
BAC	1,000 plus 1,000 plus 1,000 plus 1,000	4,000	Our project budget is $4,000.
CV	3,250 minus 3,200	50	We are under budget by $50.
CPI	3,250 divided by 3,200	1.016	We are getting 1.016 dollars out of every dollar we put into the project.
SV	3,250 minus 3,000	250	We are ahead of schedule.
SPI	3,250 divided by 3,000	1.083	We are progressing at 108% of the rate planned.
EAC	4,000 divided by 1.016	3,937	We currently estimate that the total project will cost $3,937.
ETC	3,937 minus 3,200	737	We need to spend $737 to finish the project.
VAC	4,000 minus 3,937	63	We currently expect to be $63 under budget when the project is completed.

NOTE: If your answers differ, check your rounding. It is best to round to three decimal points.

© May 2000 (Registered) Rita Mulcahy, PMP at RMC – Project Management
PHONE: (612) 929-7539, EMAIL: rita@rmcproject.com, WEB: rmcproject.com

ACCURACY OF ESTIMATES: The PMBOK® talks about three types of estimates. These often come up on the exam but are easy to answer once you memorize the figures.

1. **ORDER OF MAGNITUDE ESTIMATE:** -25% to +75%. This type of estimate is usually made during the Initiation Phase. (This is an example of the "life cycle related" questions.)
2. **BUDGET ESTIMATE**: -10% to +25%. This type of estimate is usually made during the Planning Phase.
3. **DEFINITIVE ESTIMATE**: -5% to +10%. This type of estimate is also made during the Planning Phase.

Project managers should watch out for number three. We have already said the project manager should create the project time and cost estimates, not senior management. Most project managers wish this would always be true because they are tired of dealing with unrealistic schedules and estimates. However, project managers should note the difficulty of estimating within -5% and +10% of actual.

ACCOUNTING STANDARDS: After years of helping people pass the exam, I have discovered that many things are not mentioned in the PMBOK® but are included on the test. Many of these items are cost-related questions. Only present value shows up in more than one question. So read these but do not worry. Remember that you do not have to be an accountant to pass this exam.

PRESENT VALUE: PLEASE NOTE: this topic is not on the exam very frequently. If it is on your exam, it will just be one or two questions. The amount of material presented on present value and net present value does not indicate the importance of the topic.

Present value means the value today of future cash flows. You should know the formula and be able to calculate present value, so a little practice is in order.

$$PV = \frac{FV}{(1+r)^n}$$

FV = future value
R = interest rate
N= number of time periods

In a simple example, let's ask what is the present value of US $300,000 received three years from now if we expect the interest rate to be 10%? To answer this question, it is important for you to test yourself to see if you understand the concept. Therefore, should the answer be more or less than US $300,000?

The answer is less. I can put an amount of money less than US $300,000 in the bank and in three years have US $300,000.

To solve the problem: $300/(1 + .1)^3$ equals, 300/1.331, equals US $225,394.

Exercise:

INSTRUCTIONS: Try solving a few more by completing the information in the boxes below.

Time period	Amount	Present value at 10% interest rate
1	50	
2	100	
3	300	

Answer:

Time period	Amount	Present value at 10% interest rate
1	50	45
2	100	83
3	300	225

NET PRESENT VALUE (NPV): This means the total benefits (income or revenue) less the costs. To calculate NPV you need to calculate the present value of each of the income and revenue figures and then add up the present values.

Exercise:

INSTRUCTIONS: Calculate the Net Present Value (NPV).

Time period	Income or Revenue	Present value at 10% interest rate	Costs	Present value at 10% interest rate
0	0		200	
1	50		100	
2	100		0	
3	300		0	
TOTAL				

Answer:

Time period	Income or Revenue	Present value at 10% interest rate	Costs	Present value at 10% interest rate
0	0	0	200	200
1	50	45	100	91
2	100	83	0	0
3	300	225	0	0
TOTAL		353		291

NPV = 353-291 = 62

You should not need to calculate NPV for the exam, but you must understand what it means.

You have two projects to choose from. Project A will take six years to complete and has an NPV of US $45,000 and Project B will take three years to complete and has an NPV of US $85,000. Which one would you prefer?

The answer is Project B.

INTERNAL RATE OF RETURN (IRR): To explain this concept, think of a bank account. You put money in a bank account and expect to get a return of 2% in the USA. You can think of a project in the same way. If a company has more than one project in which to invest, the company may look at the project's return and then select the highest one. If you understand this concept, you should do fine on the exam.

IRR does get confusing when you give it a formal definition. DEFINITION – *The rate (read it as interest rate) at which the project inflows (revenues) and project outflows (costs) are equal.* Calculating IRR is complex and requires the aid of a computer. You will not have do perform any IRR calculations on the exam. You will need to know the definition and be able to answer questions like the following:

You have two projects to choose from, Project A with an IRR of 21% or Project B with an IRR of 15%. Which one would you prefer?

The answer is Project A

PHONE: (612) 929-7539, EMAIL: rita@rmcproject.com, WEB: rmcproject.com

PAYBACK PERIOD: The number of time periods it takes to recover your investment in the project before you start generating revenues. For example:

> *You have two projects to choose from, Project A with a payback period of 6 months or Project B with a payback period of 18 months. Which one would you prefer?*

> *The answer is Project A.*

BENEFIT COST RATIO (BCR): Compares the costs to the benefits of different projects. A BCR of >1 means the benefits are greater than the costs. A BCR of <1 means the costs are greater than the benefits. A BCR = 1 means the costs and benefits are the same.

> *If the BCR of project A is 2.3 and the BCR of project B is 1.70, which project would you select?*

> *The answer is A, the project with the higher BCR.*

OPPORTUNITY COST: The opportunity given up by selecting one project over another. Note: this does not require any calculation. See the example below.

> *You have two projects to choose from, Project A with an NPV of US $45,000 or Project B with an NPV of US $85,000. What is the opportunity cost of selecting project B?*

> *The answer is US $45,000.*

Exercise Accounting Standards:

<u>INSTRUCTIONS</u>: Test yourself! For each row of the following chart, enter the letter of the project you would select if the following information were provided.

	Project A	Project B	Which Would You Pick?
Net Present V	$95,000	$75,000	
IRR	13%	17%	
Payback Period	16 months	21 months	
Benefit Cost Ratio	2.79	1.3	

Answer:

	Project A	Project B	Which Project Would You Pick?
Net Present V	$95,000	$75,000	A
IRR	13%	17%	B
Payback Period	16 months	21 months	A
Benefit Cost Ratio	2.79	1.3	A

SUNK COSTS: Expended costs. People unfamiliar with accounting standards might have trouble with the following question:

You have a project with an initial budget of US $1,000,000. You are halfway through the project and have spent US $2,000,000. Do you consider the US $1,000,000 over budget when determining whether to continue with the project?

The answer is no! Be aware that accounting standards say that sunk costs should not be considered when deciding whether to continue with a troubled project.

LAW OF DIMINISHING RETURNS: The more you put into something, the less you get out of it. For example, adding twice as many resources to a task may not get the task done in half the time.

WORKING CAPITAL: Current assets minus current liabilities, or the amount of money the company has to invest, including investment in projects.

PROJECT SELECTION TECHNIQUES: The following items were described above and also are considered techniques to help select the projects that will be undertaken:
- Present value
- Net present value
- IRR
- Payback period
- Benefit Cost Ratio

TYPES OF COSTS: There are several ways to look at costs when creating a budget. Feedback from people taking the exam indicates that it is difficult to differentiate between these types of costs. Therefore, it would be wise to spend time studying these types of costs even though only about three questions on the exam reference them. The examples below should help you answer questions about these types of costs.

- **VARIABLE COST** – Any costs that change with the amount of production or the amount of work. Examples include the cost of material, supplies, and wages.

- **FIXED COSTS** – Non-recurring costs that do not change as production changes. Examples include set up, rental, etc.

- **DIRECT COSTS** – Costs that are directly attributable to the work on the project. Examples are team travel, team wages, recognition, and costs of material used on the project.

- **INDIRECT COSTS** – Overhead items or costs incurred for the benefit of more than one project. Examples include taxes, fringe benefits, and janitorial services.

DEPRECIATION: Large assets (e.g., equipment) purchased by a company lose value over time. Accounting standards call this depreciation. Several methods are used to account for depreciation. The exam asks you what they are. You do not have to perform any calculations. (See, I told you I could make this easy for you!) The following information is all you need to know.

There are two forms of depreciation:
1. **STRAIGHT LINE DEPRECIATION** – The same amount of depreciation is taken each year.

> EXAMPLE: A US $1,000 item with a ten-year useful life and no salvage value (how much the item is worth at the end of its life) would be depreciated at US $100 per year.

2. **ACCELERATED DEPRECIATION** – For the exam you only need to know:
   - There are two forms of accelerated depreciation – Double Declining Balance and Sum of the Years Digits.
   - They depreciate faster than straight line.
   - You do not have to know what these two forms mean or do any calculations.

> EXAMPLE: A $1,000 item with a ten-year useful life and no salvage value (how much the item is worth at the end of its life) would be depreciated at $180 the first year, $150 the second, $130 the next, etc.

LIFE CYCLE COSTING: This is an interesting concept that slips into the exam every once in a while. The project we are working on has a life after it is completed. The project manager and the company want the project costs to be as low as possible. However, if the project manager does not consider the life cycle costs, project costs may be low at the expense of greater overall costs for the rest of the life of the project – the operations and maintenance phase. By including this concept on the exam, PMI® is effectively warning us that we should look at and manage life cycle costs instead of just project costs. This is illustrated by the following graphic.

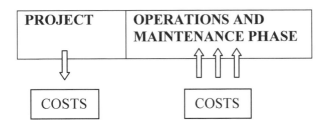

VALUE ANALYSIS: (Sometimes referred to as value engineering in the real world.) Find a less costly way to do the same scope of work. It requires the systematic use of techniques to identify the required project functions, assign values to these functions, and provide functions at the lowest overall cost without loss of performance.

SAMPLE QUESTIONS
Cost Management

	3rd Time	2nd Time	1st Time

1) Present value is:
- A. The value of assets that a company owns
- B. The value today of future cash flows
- C. The future value of money on hand today
- D. Designated by a percent

2) One common way to compute EAC is to take the BAC and.
- A. Divide by SPI
- B. Multiply by SPI
- C. Multiply by CPI
- D. Divide by CPI

3) EAC is a periodic evaluation of:
- A. Cost of work completed
- B. Value of work performed
- C. Anticipated total cost at project completion
- D. What it will cost to finish the job

4) If BCWP = 350, ACWP = 400, BCWS = 325, what is CV?
- A. 25
- B. –25
- C. 50
- D. –50

5) Rearranging resources so that a constant number of resources are used each month is called:
- A. Crashing
- B. Floating
- C. Leveling
- D. Fast tracking

6) Double declining balance is a form of:
- A. Decelerated depreciation
- B. Straight line depreciation
- C. Accelerated depreciation
- D. Life cycle costing

7) Analogous estimating:
   A. Uses bottom-up estimating techniques
   B. Is used most frequently during the Execution Phase of the project
   C. Uses top-down estimating techniques
   D. Uses actual detailed historical costs

8) The cost of choosing one project and giving up another is called:
   A. Fixed
   B. Sunk
   C. NPV
   D. Opportunity

9) The main focus of life cycle costing is to:
   A. Estimate installation costs
   B. Estimate the cost of operation and maintenance
   C. Consider installation costs when planning the project costs
   D. Consider operation and maintenance costs when planning the project costs

10) The present value of US $300,000 received 5 years from now is:
   A. US $ 204,918
   B. US $ 378,210
   C. US $ 225,890
   D. Not enough data

11) A CPI of .89 means:
   A. As of now we expect the total project to cost 89% more than planned
   B. When the project is completed we will have spent 89% more
   C. Your project is only progressing at 89% of that planned
   D. Your project is only getting 89 cents out of every dollar invested

12) An SPI of .76 means:
   A. You are over budget
   B. You are ahead of schedule
   C. You are only progressing at 76% of the rate originally planned
   D. You are only progressing at 24% of the rate originally planned

13) Which of the following is not needed in order to come up with a project estimate?
   A. WBS
   B. Network Diagram
   C. Risks
   D. Change control procedure

14) During the execution of a project, a large number of changes are made to the project. The project manager should:
   A. Wait until all changes are known and print out a new schedule
   B. Make changes as needed but retain the schedule baseline
   C. Make changes as needed
   D. Talk to management before any changes are made

15) A benefit of analogous estimating is:
   A. Estimates will be closer to what the work will actually require
   B. They are based on a detailed understanding of what the work requires
   C. Gives the project team an understanding of management's expectations
   D. Helps the project manager determine if the project will meet the schedule

16) Which of the following is an example of a parametric estimate?
   A. Regression analysis
   B. Learning bend
   C. Bottom up
   D. CPM

17) An order of magnitude estimate is made during which project management phase?
   A. Planning
   B. Close-out
   C. Execution
   D. Initiation

18) How close to actual costs would a budget estimate expect to be?
   A. −75% to +25%
   B. −10% to +25%
   C. +10% to −25%
   D. −5% to +10%

19) Which of the following factors would you not consider when choosing which of two projects will be undertaken?
   A. NPV
   B. BCR
   C. Payback period
   D. Law of diminishing returns

20) If the NPV is $30,000 for project A and $50,000 for project B, what is the opportunity cost if project B is selected?
   A. $23,000
   B. $30,000
   C. $20,000
   D. $50,000

21) During the allocation of project costs a project manager is trying to decide where to allocate team training. Such an expense should be considered:
   A.   Direct costs
   B.   NPV
   C.   Indirect cost
   D.   Variable cost

22) Setup costs are an example of:
   A.   Variable costs
   B.   Fixed costs
   C.   Direct costs
   D.   Indirect costs

23) A contractor has just received the procurement documents for a new project and notices a value analysis clause. What is the benefit of value analysis?
   A.   To get more value from the cost analysis
   B.   To get management to buy into the project
   C.   To get the team to buy into the project
   D.   To find a less costly way of doing the same scope of work

24) Who has the cost risk in a fixed price contract?
   A.   The team
   B.   Buyer
   C.   Seller
   D.   Management

25) The contractor tells you that your activities have resulted in an increase in their costs. You should:
   A.   Issue a change to the project costs
   B.   Have a meeting with management
   C.   Ask the contractor for supporting information
   D.   Deny any wrong doing

26) A project manager has a troubled project. There have been delays, conflicts, and lots of changes. During a performance analysis the project manager's analysis shows that she will have a cost overrun at the end of the project. If you were her you would:
   A.   Evaluate options
   B.   Meet with management
   C.   Meet with the team
   D.   Change the project plan

27) What is earned value?
   A. BCWP
   B. BCWS
   C. ACWP
   D. ACWS

ANSWERS
1 B
2 D
3 C
4 D
5 C
6 C
7 C
8 D
9 D
10 D
11 D
12 C
13 D
14 B
15 C
16 A
17 D
18 B
19 D
20 B
21 A
22 B
23 D
24 C
25 C
26 A
27 A

Time and Cost Game

The Time and Cost questions tend to be the most difficult for many people. To improve your ability to correctly answer these questions, I have created the following game.

When preparing for the exam, I have found it best to have students answer questions in writing AND verbally. This combination gives people a chance to better access memory patterns and thereby remember the material. This game is a verbal game and should be done with more than one person. The second person can be a spouse, child, or someone else studying for the PMP® exam. I have even used this game in a room of 30 people and given prizes to the person with the most questions right. If you are studying alone, simply put your hand over the answers.

INSTRUCTIONS: Cut out the cards along the lines provided. Try to answer as many questions as you can in 10 minutes. If you answer 10 questions correctly in ten minutes, this should prove to you that you would not have a time problem taking the exam. (The exam allows over 1½ minutes per question.) Obviously, this exercise will also give you a chance to test your understanding. GOOD LUCK!

- FOR ONE PARTICIPANT: Cover the answers.

- FOR TWO PARTICIPANTS: One person asks the questions and the other answers.

- FOR MORE THAN TWO PARTICIPANTS: One person asks the questions and the others answer. One of those answering should also keep track of the number of correct answers.

Q – What type of network diagrams can be drawn with an activity-on-line diagram?	Q – What type of network diagram would use optimistic time estimates?
A – PERT and CPM	A – PERT
Q – The critical path is?	Q – What is the PERT formula?
A – The longest path in the network.	A – (P + 4M +O)/6
Q What type of network diagramming method uses dummy activities?	Q – What does a finish-to-start relationship mean?
A – PERT and CPM	A – One task must finish before the next can start.
Q – Why would you want to crash a network diagram?	Q – Name one of the differences between bar charts and network diagrams.
A – To shorten the project duration.	A – Bar charts do not show logical relationships between activities.
Q – What does a milestone chart show?	Q – What is the duration of a milestone?
A – Significant events on the project.	A – Zero

Q – "How much work should be done" has what earned value name? A – BCWS	Q – What is the earned value name for "how much you spent to date?" A – ACWP
Q – What does the schedule variance tells you? A – How much you are behind or ahead of schedule.	Q – What is the cost variance formula? A – BCWP - ACWP
Q – What does the estimate at completion tell you? A – What we now expect the total project to cost.	Q – What does present value mean? A – The value today of future cash flows.
Q – What are sunk costs? A – Expended costs.	Q – What does a BCR of 2.5 mean? A – The benefits are 2 ½ times the costs.
Q – What is analogous estimating? A – Top-down estimating.	Q – What is the range of accuracy with a budget estimate? A – (-10% to +25%)

Q – What are fixed costs? A – Costs that do not change with project activity.	Q – What are direct costs? A – Costs incurred directly by the project.
Q – What is value analysis? A – Finding a less costly way to complete the work without affecting quality.	Q – What is a management reserve? A – A "pot" of time or money held for risks.
Q – Cost risk is greater for the buyer in what type of contract? A – CPFF	Q – What is a heuristic? A – Rule of thumb
Q – Define slack. A – The amount of time an activity can be delayed without delaying the project.	Q – Why would a project manager want to perform resource leveling? A – To smooth the peaks and valleys of monthly resource usage consumed by the project.
Q – A critical path task will have how much slack? A – Zero	Q – What is parametric estimating? A – Using mathematical relationships to create estimates (e.g., dollars per foot).

Quality Management
(PMBOK® Chapter 8)

Quality-related questions can be confusing because PMI® espouses a quality philosophy that may be different than your company's. Read the PMBOK® Quality chapter and this chapter carefully and memorize the definitions provided. Many of my students report that the definitions are extremely important for the exam. There may be fifteen questions that relate to control charts and definitions.

HOT TOPICS in order of importance:
- Control charts
  - Control limits
  - Assignable cause
  - Rule of seven
  - Specification limits
  - Three sigma
  - Six sigma
  - Normal dist. curve
  - "Out of control"
- Prevention over inspection
- Quality philosophy
- Quality
- Quality planning
- Quality assurance
- Quality control
- Pareto diagrams
- Gold plating
- Total quality management
- Quality control tools
- Checklists
- ISO 9000
- Continuous improvement
- Marginal analysis
- Responsibility for quality
- Impact of poor quality
- Cost of conformance and non-conformance
- Statistics
  - Normal distribution
  - Population
  - Sample
  - Variable
  - Attribute
  - Probability
  - Statistical independence
  - Mutual exclusivity
- Fishbone diagrams
- Cost benefit analysis
- Benchmarking
- Flow charts
- Just in time
- Design of experiments

QUALITY PHILOSOPHY: I list this as a separate item to make sure you notice it. You must understand PMI®'s approach to quality because it is different from what most people have learned. PMI®'s philosophy can be illustrated in the definitions of quality, gold plating, and prevention over inspection.

QUALITY: *CONFORMANCE TO REQUIREMENTS, SPECIFICATIONS, AND FITNESS OF USE.* This one phrase should help you answer about four questions because it shows up in many different ways. Memorize it!

The definition of quality ties into what I mentioned in Framework under the definition of stakeholder. PMI®'s approach to quality is that the project manager should perform careful and accurate needs analysis at the beginning of the project to ensure stakeholder satisfaction. These requirements become the foundation of the scope of work.

The project manager's role during the project is to simply complete what has been committed. Notice that quality is NOT giving the customer extra. PMI®'s philosophy is that quality is doing what you said you were going to do.

GOLD PLATING: PMI® does not recommend giving the customer extras (e.g., extra functionality, higher-quality components, extra scope of work or better performance). Gold plating adds no value to the project. Often such additions are included based on the project team's impression of what the customer would like. This impression may not be accurate. Considering that only 26% of all projects succeed, project managers would be better off spending their time conforming to requirements.

DEFINITION OF QUALITY MANAGEMENT (page 83): "The processes required to ensure that the project will satisfy the needs for which it was undertaken." This can also mean the same thing as completing the project with no deviations from the project requirements. In the PMBOK® quality management includes quality planning, quality assurance and quality control.

CONTINUOUS IMPROVEMENT or KAIZEN: Small improvements in products or processes to reduce costs and ensure consistency of performance of products or services. These two words are taken to mean the same thing on the exam, however, in Japan this is just a word not a quality movement. Kaizen means Kai (alter) and Zen (make better or improve). In the United States and most of Western Europe, improvements are thought of as BIG improvements. In Japan improvements are thought of as small improvements.

MARGINAL ANALYSIS: Optimal quality is reached at the point where the incremental revenue from improvement equals the incremental cost to secure it.

JUST IN TIME (JIT): This is an approach to decrease the amount of inventory that a company carries and therefore decrease the investment in inventory. A just in time philosophy requires a company to improve quality (forces quality) because extra materials are not available.

ISO 9000: A standard created by the International Standards Organization (ISO) to help ensure that organizations follow their own quality procedures. Many people think that ISO 9000 tells you what quality should be or describes a recommended quality system. This is not correct. This problem has shown up on the exam, making the correct answer actually untrue. Please see question 5 in the sample exam at the end of the chapter.

TOTAL QUALITY MANAGEMENT (TQM): A philosophy that encourages companies and their employees to focus on finding ways to continuously improve the quality of their business practices and products.

STATISTICS: Remember all those statistics you still want to forget? Well, they are on the exam. Thankfully, there are probably only three questions on this topic as a whole. The following should refresh your memory and make the questions easier for you.

> NORMAL DISTRIBUTION: A normal distribution is the most common probability distribution and is used to measure variations. Standard deviation (or sigma) is a measure of how far you are from the mean (the dotted vertical line). NOTE: Remember the formula for standard deviation using optimistic, pessimistic, and most likely estimates is: $(P - O)/6$.

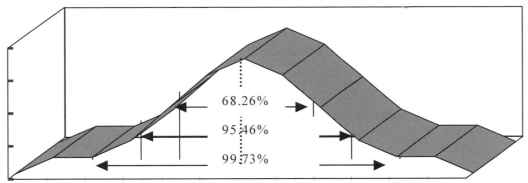

NORMAL CURVE

3 OR 6 SIGMA: Sigma is another name for standard deviation. 3 or 6 sigma represents the level of quality that a company has decided to try to achieve. At 6 sigma, only 1 out of 1,000 widgets produced have a problem. At 3 sigma, 27 out of 1,000 will have a problem. Therefore, 6 sigma represents a higher quality standard than 3 sigma.3 or 6 sigma are also used to calculate the upper and lower control limits in a control chart, described later.

You should memorize:

- +/- 1 sigma is equal to 68.26%

- +/- 2 sigma equals 95.46% and

- +/- 3 sigma equals 99.73%

- +/- 6 sigma equals 99.99%

OTHER STATISTICS TO KNOW (page 87): Here is a primer, or memory jogger, of some of the other statistics that have appeared on the exam and that you probably already know.
- **POPULATION** – The entire universe, for example, all women over age 30.
- **SAMPLE** – A part of the population. It is best to take a sample of a population if studying the entire population would (these have all appeared on the exam):
  - Take too long
  - Cost too much
  - Be too destructive
  - When the cost of 100% inspection is too high
  - When we believe there are not many defects
- **VARIABLE** – The characteristic you want to measure (e.g., size, shape, weight).
- **ATTRIBUTE** – The measurement (inches, pounds) that will tell if the sample is acceptable. Attributes can be subjective or objective and are the specific characteristics for which a product is built.
- **PROBABILITY** – The likelihood that something will occur.
- **STATISTICAL INDEPENDENCE** – The probability of one event occurring does not affect the probability of another event occurring (e.g., the probability of rolling a 6 on a die is statistically independent from the probability of rolling a 5 on the next roll).
- **MUTUALLY EXCLUSIVE** – Two events are said to be mutually exclusive if they cannot both occur in a single trial. For example, flipping a coin once cannot result in both a head and a tail.

RESPONSIBILITY FOR QUALITY: The entire organization has responsibilities relating to quality. Therefore read questions on this topic carefully to interpret about whom in the organization the question is asking. PMI® is notorious for these troublesome questions so you can expect them to be on the exam. I have other tricks for you that will help make this easier:

- When the question asks who has the ULTIMATE responsibility for quality, the answer is the employee.
- When the question asks who has the OVERALL or PRIMARY responsibility for quality, the answer is the project manager.
- When the question asks who has the PRIMARY RESPONSIBILITY FOR ESTABLISHING DESIGN AND TEST SPECIFICATIONS, the answer is the engineer. Remember that this is a project management exam, not a quality professional exam. Only once have I heard about a question on the exam that referred to the quality specialist or engineer.

IMPACT OF POOR QUALITY: Some questions are easy to answer, such as this one. If you have poor quality, you have:
- Increased costs
- Low morale
- Lower customer satisfaction
- Increased risk

Increases in quality can result in:
- Increased productivity
- Increased cost effectiveness
- Decreased cost risk

PREVENTION OVER INSPECTION: Prevention over inspection and the quality philosophy flow through many of the questions on the exam. Many years ago, the main focus of quality was on inspection (e.g., check production after items are produced). The cost of doing so (cost of non-conformance mentioned later) are so high that it is better to spend money preventing problems with quality. QUALITY MUST BE PLANNED IN NOT INSPECTED IN! This is part of PMI®'s quality philosophy and frequently comes up on the exam.

COST OF CONFORMANCE/NON-CONFORMANCE: PMI® and Deming (an expounder of quality philosophy) say that 85% of the costs of quality are the direct responsibility of management. Specifically these costs are:

COST OF CONFORMANCE	COST OF NON-CONFORMANCE
Quality training	Rework
Studies	Scrap
Surveys	Inventory costs
	Warranty costs

QUALITY PLANNING (page 85), QUALITY ASSURANCE (page 88), QUALITY CONTROL (page 89): There are usually many questions on the exam that require you to know the difference between these components of quality. Please refer to the PMBOK®. Many people find it hard to understand the difference, so the following table includes some important tricks to tell them apart.

Tricks to understand the difference	Quality Planning	Quality Assurance	Quality Control
	Plan	Implement	Check
	Determine what will be quality on the project and how quality will be measured	Determine if your measurement of quality is appropriate	Perform the measurement and compare to the quality plan
Do during	Planning	Execution	Control

QUALITY PLANNING (page 85) – Quality planning is done concurrently with other project planning. In addition to the chart above, quality planning includes:

- Identifying which quality standards are relevant to the project and determining how to satisfy them
- **BENCHMARKING** – Looking at past projects to determine ideas for improvement and to provide a measure of quality performance
- **COST BENEFIT ANALYSIS** – Considering the benefits versus the costs of quality requirements
- **FLOWCHARTS** (page 86, 87) Showing how a process or system flows from beginning to end and how the elements interrelate. It is used in quality planning to analyze potential future quality problems and determine quality standards. It is used in quality control to analyze quality problems. A fishbone diagram is also an example of a flow chart.
- **DESIGN OF EXPERIMENTS** (page 87) – The use of experimentation or "what if" to determine what variables will improve quality.

QUALITY ASSURANCE (page 88) – Quality assurance is primarily done during the execution phase of the project. In addition to the chart above, quality assurance includes:

- The process of evaluating overall performance on a regular basis to provide confidence that the project will satisfy the relevant quality standards
- **QUALITY AUDITS** (page 88) – A structured review of quality activities that identifies lessons learned

QUALITY CONTROL (page 89) – Quality control is done during the control phase of the project. In addition to the chart above, quality control includes:

- The process of monitoring specific project results to determine if they comply with relevant quality standards and identify ways to eliminate causes of unsatisfactory performance
- Performance of the measurement or process, using quality control tools or checking the work
- **QUALITY CONTROL TOOLS** – As described below

TRICK: It is easier to determine if something is part of quality control (e.g., relates to one of the quality control tools) than part of quality assurance. So, if a question asks, "Which of the following is done during quality assurance," determine if the item described relates to a quality control tool. If it does not, then it is part of quality assurance.

PARETO DIAGRAMS (page 90-91): Projects always run into problems. Many project managers will attempt to resolve each problem that arises. However, this may not be the best use of the project manager's time.

If a project manager were to graph the types of problems and the frequency of their occurrence, the project manager would come up with a Pareto diagram. The diagram is based on the 80/20 rule – 80% of the problems will come from 20% of the work. See PMBOK® page 91 for a picture of a Pareto chart.

The exam has used the following phrase to describe a Pareto chart; "*The chart presents the information being examined in its order of priority and helps focus attention on the most critical issues.*"

FISHBONE DIAGRAMS (also called CAUSE-AND-EFFECT or ISHIKAWA and seen on page 86): The diagram illustrates how various causes and sub-causes relate to create potential problems and looks like the bones of a fish. The exam has used the following three phrases to describe this diagram. You should memorize these:

analyze problems

1. *A creative way to look at the causes or potential causes of a problem.*
2. *Helps stimulate thinking, organizes thoughts and generates discussion.*
3. *Can be used to explore a desired future outcome and the factors to which it relates.*

The following, and PMBOK® page 86, are illustrations of a fishbone diagram.

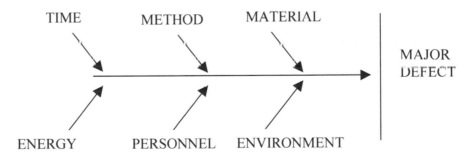

CHECKLISTS: Contain a list of items to inspect or a picture of the item to be inspected with space to note any defects found.

CONTROL CHARTS (page 90): Much of what is tested on control charts is not in the PMBOK®. You should read the following carefully and perform the following exercise. When you are able to pick out all the items in a control chart on the exercise, you should be ready to answer any exam questions about control charts.

PMI® says that control charts are "graphic displays of the results, over time, of a process...used to determine if the process is 'in control'." A manufacturer of widgets (an example often used on the exam) knows that production can never be exact. The measurement of each widget should however be within a range of normal and acceptable limits. A control chart helps monitor production and other processes to see the process is within these limits and therefore if a problem exists. The following can be found on a control chart:

UPPER AND LOWER CONTROL LIMITS – These limits are often shown as two dashed lines and show the acceptable range of variation of a process. The range is determined by the organization's quality standard (e.g., 3 or 6 sigma).

MEAN – A line in the middle of the control chart that shows the middle of the range of acceptable variation of the process.

SPECIFICATION LIMITS – Are often shown as solid lines *outside* the upper and lower control limits on the chart. They represent the customer's expectations or contractual requirements for performance and quality.

OUT OF CONTROL – The process is out of control under two circumstances:
- A data point falls outside of the upper or lower control limit
- Non-random data points are within the upper and lower control limits.

RULE OF SEVEN – Is a rule of thumb or Heuristic. It refers to non-random data points grouped together that total seven on either side of the mean. The rule of seven tell you that although none of these points are outside the control limits, they are not random, and the process is out of control. This type of situation should be investigated and a cause found.

ASSIGNABLE CAUSE – A data point that requires investigation to determine the cause of the variation.

Exercise: Control Charts

INSTRUCTIONS: Find all examples of each item listed below on one or both of the control charts shown on the next page and place its item number next to its location. If unsure, take a guess and then review the control chart descriptions on the last page. **These pictures represent two different control charts.**

NOTE: The questions on the exam relating to control charts do not use pictures but may ask questions, which are easier to answer if you can picture a control chart in you mind. Because many people have excellent visual memory, this exercise is designed to make sure you understand control charts and can answer questions about them.

Exercise: Control Charts (continued): Find the following on the charts.

1. Upper control limit
2. Lower control limit
3. Assignable cause
4. The process is out of control
5. Normal and expected variation in the process
6. Rule of seven
7. Specification limits
8. Three sigma
9. Six sigma
10. Normal distribution curve

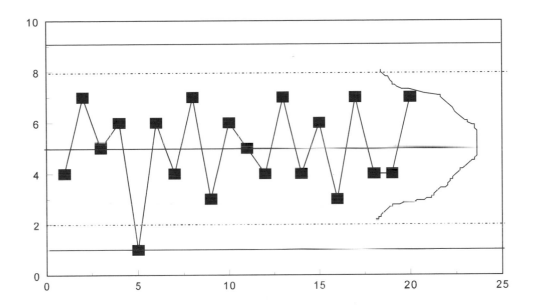

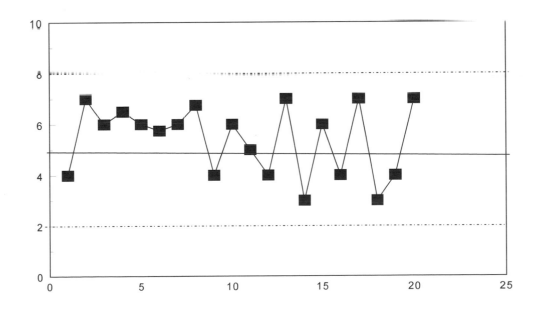

Answer: Control Charts

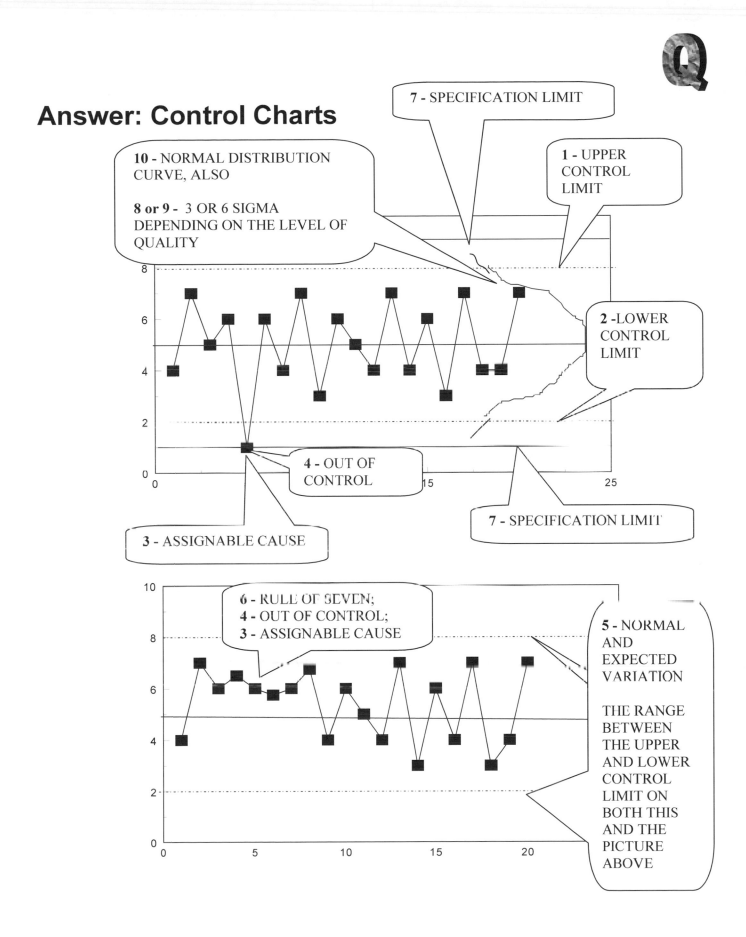

7 - SPECIFICATION LIMIT

10 - NORMAL DISTRIBUTION CURVE, ALSO

8 or 9 - 3 OR 6 SIGMA DEPENDING ON THE LEVEL OF QUALITY

1 - UPPER CONTROL LIMIT

2 -LOWER CONTROL LIMIT

4 - OUT OF CONTROL

3 - ASSIGNABLE CAUSE

7 - SPECIFICATION LIMIT

6 - RULE OF SEVEN;
4 - OUT OF CONTROL;
3 - ASSIGNABLE CAUSE

5 - NORMAL AND EXPECTED VARIATION

THE RANGE BETWEEN THE UPPER AND LOWER CONTROL LIMIT ON BOTH THIS AND THE PICTURE ABOVE

SAMPLE QUESTIONS
Quality Management

	3rd Time	2nd Time	1st Time

1) When a product or service completely meets a customer's requirements:
    A. Quality is achieved
    B. The cost of quality is high
    C. The cost of quality is low
    D. The customer pays the minimum price

2) "The concept of optimal quality level is reached at the point where the incremental revenue from product improvement equals the incremental cost to secure it" refers to?
    A. Quality control analysis
    B. Marginal analysis
    C. Standard quality analysis
    D. Conformance analysis

3) Primary responsibility for quality management in the project rests with the:
    A. Project engineer
    B. Purchasing agent
    C. Quality manager
    D. Project manager

4) Primary responsibility for establishing design and test specifications rests with:
    A. Senior management
    B. Procurement
    C. Engineering
    D. Quality control

5) ISO 9000 series is:
    A. A set of guidelines for quality
    B. A set of forms and procedures to ensure quality
    C. An international standard that describes a recommended quality system
    D. B and C

6) A project sponsor is not comfortable with the quality level of the project. He instructs the project manager to come up with quality standards and to improve quality. The project manager however is concerned about the effect of quality improvements on the project. Which of the following best describes the results of an increase in quality?
    A. Increased productivity, increased cost effectiveness, decreased cost risk
    B. Increased productivity, decreased cost effectiveness, and increased cost risk
    C. Reduced productivity and no change to cost effectiveness and cost risk
    D. Reduced productivity and an increase in overall product or service cost

7) From the project perspective, quality attributes:
   A. Determine how effectively the performing organization supports the project
   B. Can be subjective or objective
   C. Are specific characteristics for which a product is designed and tested
   D. B and C

8) Quality is:
   A. Conformance to the customer's needs
   B. Adding extras to make the customer happy
   C. Conformance to requirements, specifications and fitness of use
   D. Conformance to management's requirements

9) During a team meeting the team determines that the customer would benefit from a specific area of extra work and they add it to the project. This is called:
   A. Gold plating
   B. Extra scope
   C. An approved change order
   D. A good idea

10) Which of the following is an example of quality assurance?
   A. Inspection
   B. Team training
   C. Pareto diagrams
   D. Fishbone diagrams

11) A Pareto diagram helps the project manager to:
   A. Focus on the most critical issues to improve quality
   B. Focus on stimulating thinking
   C. Explore a desired future outcome
   D. Determine if a process is out of control

12) During the executions phase of the project the project manager's company begins to make use of control charts on all their projects. A control chart can help to:
   A. Focus on the most critical issues to improve quality
   B. Focus on stimulating thinking
   C. Explore a desired future outcome
   D. Determine if a process is out of control

13) A sample of a population is taken when testing the entire population would __:
   A. Take too long
   B. Be too inexpensive
   C. Be mutually exclusive
   D. Show many defects

14) Which of the following is an example of the cost of conformance to quality?
   A. Rework
   B. Quality training
   C. Scrap
   D. Warranty costs

15) What is the meaning of standard deviation?
   A. A measure of how far you are from the average estimate
   B. A measure of how far you are from the mean
   C. A measure of how correct the sample is
   D. A measure of how much time remains in the project

16) Three sigmas from the mean are equal to?
   A. 68.26%
   B. 99.9%
   C. 95.4%
   D. 99.7%

17) Which of the following is not an example of a variable?
   A. Size
   B. Shape
   C. Pounds
   D. Weight

18) A control chart shows seven data points on one side of the mean. What should be done?
   A. Nothing, this is not a problem
   B. Tell the customer
   C. Investigate and find an assignable cause
   D. This is just the rule of seven and can be ignored

19) What is the inventory on hand in a Just in Time (JIT) environment?
   A. 45%
   B. 10%
   C. 12%
   D. 0%

20) An Ishikawa diagram helps _____:
   A. Explore past outcomes
   B. Stimulate thinking, organize thoughts and generate discussion
   C. Show team responsibilities
   D. Show functional responsibilities

21) In project management, the importance of quality compared to cost and schedule is:
   A. Cost is most important, quality next and then schedule
   B. Quality is more important than either
   C. Schedule is most important, quality next, and then cost
   D. All three are equal

© May 2000 (Registered) Rita Mulcahy, PMP at RMC – Project Management

PHONE: (612) 929-7539, EMAIL: rita@rmcproject.com, WEB: rmcproject.com

It is illegal to copy, transmit, or reproduce any part of this document without specific written approval from the author!

106

ANSWERS

1 A
2 B
3 D
4 C
5 C
6 A
7 D
8 C
9 A
10 B
11 A
12 D
13 A
14 B
15 B
16 D
17 C
18 C
19 D
20 B
21 D

Chapter 8

Human Resource Management
(PMBOK® Chapter 9)

These are probably the easiest questions on the exam! However you may want to read *Principles of Project Management* and this chapter in the PMBOK®.

PMI® splits human resources into administrative and behavioral management topics. Most of the answers to human resource questions should come from your everyday knowledge and work experience. You are required to know that people must be compensated for their work (I am serious, this question has appeared on the exam) and that people should be rewarded. There are only a few things that I need to explain or clarify.

HOT TOPICS in order of importance:
• Roles and responsibilities
• Powers of the project manager
– Formal
– Reward
– Penalty
– Expert
– Referent
• Conflict management
• 7 sources of conflict
• Conflict resolution techniques
– Problem solving
– Compromising
– Withdrawal
– Smoothing
– Forcing
• Motivation theory
– Maslow
– Theory X, Y
– Herzberg
• Responsibility charts
• Team building
• Leadership skills
• Miscellaneous terms
– Constraints
– Arbitration
– Perquisites
– Fringe benefits
– Expectancy theory
– Halo effect
– War room

ROLES AND RESPONSIBILITIES: There can be many questions on the exam regarding who is responsible for what activities relating to project management. This topic is addressed throughout this book and is important to understand for the exam. The following is an overview of the concept. Take note, this topic contains many PMI®-isms.

Many project managers in the workplace are handed a project, schedule and budget with which to work. This is not acceptable project management. Because a project manager is the only one with the skills to plan, estimate, and schedule a project using modern project management techniques, PMI® states that it is the project manager's responsibility to plan, estimate, and schedule a project. Some of the primary reasons projects fail relate to this issue and are:

- The project is defined without the project manager's assistance.
- Unrealistic time frames.
- Senior management meddling.

It is the team's role to help plan what needs to be done (WBS), how the project will flow from beginning to end (Network Diagram), as well as to estimate times for their tasks. Team members must then concentrate on completing their tasks.

It is senior management's role (those who manage project managers) to approve the OVERALL Project Plan, budget, and schedule and to approve any changes that are made to these overall figures. Senior management must assign a project manager at the onset of the project, empower the project manager, and protect the project from outside influences.

To determine who is responsible for which project management activities on the exam, remember that the person experiencing the problem must solve it themselves, not run to someone senior.

There are many situational questions on the exam. Although they may seem wordy, if you cut down to the essence of the question, they are really quite simple. Many such questions ask who is responsible for what on the project. Test your understanding with the next exercise.

Exercise: Test yourself! Considering the previous comments, write the initials of who has the primary responsibility to solve each problem in the following chart. The choices are team member (T), project manager (PM), senior management (SM). HINT: As most projects are managed in matrix forms of organization, keep matrix organizations in mind when considering these situations.

	Situation	Who solves the problem?
1	Two project team members are having a disagreement.	
2	There is a change to the overall project deliverable.	
3	A boss is trying to pull a team member off the project to do other work.	
4	The project manager does not have the authority to get things done.	
5	There are not enough resources to complete the project.	
6	The team is unsure of what needs to happen when.	
7	A task needs more time and will cause the project to be delayed.	
8	A task needs more time without causing the project to be delayed.	
9	A team member is not performing.	
10	The team is not sure who is in charge of the project.	
11	There is talk that the project may no longer be needed.	
12	Senior management provides an unrealistic schedule requirement.	
13	The team is in conflict over priorities between tasks	
14	The project is behind schedule.	
15	A team member determines that another method is needed to complete the task within its scope of work.	

Answer: This exercise is designed to check your understanding of who is responsible for what on the project. If you got many of the answers wrong, then you should re-read the Roles and Responsibilities topic above and the exact wording of the situations presented here. Keep in mind that in this exercise, there are no "correct" answers. They are all subject to interpretation of the situation.

	Situation	Who Solves the Problem?
1	Two project team members are having a disagreement – *The person involved in the conflict must solve it themselves.*	T
2	There is a change to the overall project deliverable – *This is a change to the charter. Only senior management can approve changes to the charter.*	SM
3	A boss is trying to pull a team member off the project to do other work – *The project manager must give the team member enough information (e.g., Gantt chart, network diagram, project plan, risks) so that they can manage their own workload.*	T
4	The project manager does not have the authority to get things done – *It is senior management's role to give the project manager authority in the form of a charter.*	SM
5	There are not enough resources to complete the project– *Senior management and functional management control resources.*	SM
6	The team is unsure of what needs to happen when – *It is the project manager's role to take the individual tasks and task estimates and combine them into the project schedule.*	PM
7	A task needs more time and will cause the project to be delayed – *Any such changes are changes to the charter and require senior management involvement.*	SM
8	A task needs more time without causing the project to be delayed – *It is the project manager's role to manage the project time and cost reserves to handle any such eventuality.*	PM
9	A team member is not performing – *Senior management and functional management control resources.*	SM
10	The team is not sure who is in charge of the project – *Senior management designates the project manager in the charter.*	SM
11	There is talk that the project may no longer be needed – *It is senior management's role to protect the project from changes, including such a large change.*	SM
12	Senior management provides an unrealistic schedule requirement – *Although it is often the senior manager's fault that this occurs, only they can make a change to the charter (including schedule requirements). The project manager must provide evidence that the schedule is unrealistic.*	SM
13	The team is in conflict over priorities between tasks – *It is the project manager's role to settle any such conflicts and to provide a project network diagram and critical path.*	PM
14	The project is behind schedule – *Only the project manager can control the overall project schedule. During execution, the team focuses on completing their tasks.*	PM
15	A team member determines that another method is needed to complete the task within its scope of work – *The team member has control over their tasks as long as they meet the time, quality, cost, and scope of work objectives set up with the PM.*	T

POWERS OF THE PROJECT MANAGER (Principles page 75): Many people have told me that they find it surprising that this topic is on the exam. In fact it is not surprising. Project managers almost always have difficulty getting people to cooperate and perform, especially if they are working in a matrix organization. Therefore, it is important for the project manager to know what they can do to get people to perform. These are the "powers."

- **FORMAL** (legitimate) – Power based on your position.
  "Do the work because I have been put in charge!"

- **REWARD** – Giving rewards.
  "I know that you have been wanting to participate in the acceptance testing of this project. Because of your performance, I will assign you as part of that team!"

- **PENALTY** (coercive) – Being able to penalize team members.
  "If this does not get done on time, I will remove you from the group going to Hawaii for the customer meeting!"

- **EXPERT** – Being the technical or project management expert.
  "We should listen to what the project manager suggests. She is the world's authority on this technology!"

- **REFERENT** – Referring to the authority of someone in a higher position.
  "The senior vice-president has put me in charge of this project. We will therefore do it this way!"

NOTE: PMI® says that the best forms of power are EXPERT and REWARD. Penalty is the worst. PMI® also says that FORMAL, REWARD, and PENALTY are powers derived from the project manager's position in the company. EXPERT power is earned on your own.

CONFLICT MANAGEMENT: Although many of us think conflict is bad, it actually presents opportunity for the project to improve. This is another situation where the understanding of many project managers differs from accepted research. Read this carefully.

Changing Views of Conflict	
Old	**New**
Conflict is dysfunctional and caused by personality differences or a failure of leadership.	Conflict is an inevitable consequence of organizational interactions.
Conflict is to be avoided.	Conflict can be beneficial.
Conflict is resolved by physical separation or the intervention of upper management.	Conflict is resolved through identifying the causes and problem solving by the people involved and their immediate manager.

Conflict is unavoidable because of the:
- Nature of projects
- Limited power of the project manager
- Necessity for obtaining resources from functional managers

Conflict can be avoided through the following techniques:
- Informing the team:
  - Exactly where the project is headed
  - Project goals and objectives
  - All key decisions
  - Changes
- Clearly assigning tasks without ambiguity or overlapping responsibilities
- Making work assignments interesting and challenging

SEVEN SOURCES OF CONFLICT (Principles page 161): Many project managers think that the main source of conflict on a project is personality differences. They may be surprised to learn that this is rarely the case. It only becomes personal if the root cause of the problem is not resolved. The *Principles* book describes seven categories of conflict and lists their actual order of frequency as:
- Schedules
- Project priorities
- Resources
- Technical opinions
- Administrative procedures
- Cost
- Personality

The exam may ask for the top sources of conflict, so it would be useful to know the top four. Since many project managers think that number 1 is personality conflict, you can expect the exam to include questions with that choice.

CONFLICT RESOLUTION TECHNIQUES (Principles page 161):
- **PROBLEM SOLVING** (CONFRONTING) – Solving the real problem. *"It seems that the real problem here is not lack of communication but lack of knowledge of what needs to be done when. Here is a copy of the project schedule. It should let you know what you need to know."*

- **COMPROMISING** – Finding solutions that bring some degree of satisfaction to both parties. *"Let us do a little of what both of you suggest."*

- **WITHDRAWAL** – Retreating or postponing a decision on a problem. *"Let's deal with this issue next week."*

- **SMOOTHING** – Emphasizing agreement rather than differences of opinion. "Let's calm down and get the job done!"

- **FORCING** – Pushing one viewpoint at the expense of another. *"Do it my way!"*

NOTE: The exam may ask you which method is best and worst. PMI® recommends problem solving as the best choice, followed by compromising. Forcing is last.

MOTIVATION THEORY: I was surprised four years ago that the exam included questions about theories of motivation until I realized that this is an important topic for gaining cooperation. Here are three theories you need to know for the exam:

MASLOW'S HIERARCHY OF NEEDS – Maslow's message is that people do not work for security or money. They work to get a chance to contribute and to use their skills. Maslow calls this "self-actualization." He created a pyramid to show how people are motivated and said that one cannot ascend to the next level until the levels below are fulfilled.

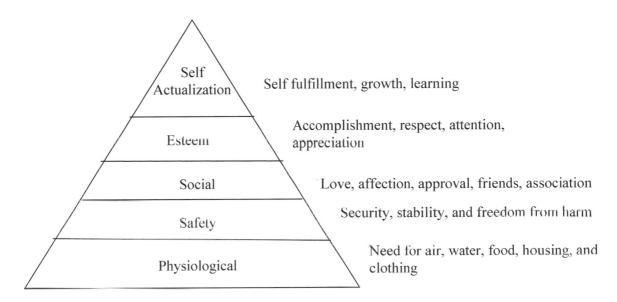

MCGREGOR'S THEORY OF X AND Y: McGregor believed that all workers could be put into one of two groups, X and Y. The exam uses many different ways to describe each of these theories. It can be confusing to determine which is the correct answer or even what the choices are saying. For all of you with visual memory, I will provide you with a foolproof method to answer any question on these theories.

THEORY X – Based on the picture, take a guess what theory X is.

People need to be watched every minute. People are incapable, avoid responsibility, and avoid work whenever possible.

THEORY Y – Based on the picture, take a guess as to what theory Y is.

People are willing to work without supervision and want to achieve. People can direct their own efforts.

HERZBERG'S THEORY – This theory deals with hygiene factors and motivating agents.

HYGIENE FACTORS – Poor hygiene factors may destroy motivation but improving them, under most circumstances, will not improve motivation. Hygiene factors are not sufficient to motivate people. Examples of these are:

- Working conditions
- Salary
- Personal life
- Relationships at work
- Security
- Status

MOTIVATING AGENTS – What motivates people is the work itself, including such things as:
- Responsibility
- Self-actualization
- Professional growth
- Recognition

The lesson to project managers - motivating people is best done by rewarding them and letting them grow. Giving raises does not do it. Many project managers initially disagreed with this in my previous classes until they had a chance to think about it. Besides, the project manager may not have any influence over pay raises if the team members do not report to the project manager in the organizational structure.

RESPONSIBILITY CHARTS (pages 96 and 97 with illustrations): PMI® advocates that all roles and responsibilities on the project be clearly assigned and closely linked to the project scope definition. Many types of charts may be used for this purpose. For the exam, you should know what is shown on each chart. For example:

A responsibility matrix does not show _____?

Answer – when people will do their jobs (time).

1. RESPONSIBILITY MATRIX (page 96) – This chart cross-references team members with the tasks they are to accomplish. For example:

TASK	TEAM MEMBER			
	Nicole	Morgan	Rikki	Alexis
A	P		S	
B		S		P

KEY- P = Primary responsibility, S = Secondary responsibility

It may also cross reference team members and issues. For example:

Issue	TEAM MEMBER			
	Nicole	Morgan	Rikki	Alexis
Invoicing	P		S	
Hardware		S		P

2. RESOURCE HISTOGRAM (page 97) – Graphs months against the number of resources used and is displayed in a bar chart format. A picture is shown in the PMBOK®.

3. RESOURCE GANTT CHART – Shows WHEN staff is allocated to tasks.

TEAM BUILDING (TEAM DEVELOPMENT pages 99-100): Questions related to team building are very easy, and most people can answer them based on their own experience. A few points need to be clarified.

- It is the job of the project manager to "enhance the ability of stakeholders to contribute as individuals as well as enhance the ability of the team to function as a team."

- Project managers should incorporate team-building activities into all project activities.

- Team building requires a concerted effort and continued attention throughout the life of the project.

- The WBS is a team building tool.

- Team building should start early in the life of the project.

LEADERSHIP SKILLS: The project manager must have the following skills and know when to use them on the project:

- Directive
- Facilitating
- Coaching
- Supportive

MISCELLANEOUS TERMS:

- **Constraints** (page 95) – Constraints are factors that limit the project team's options. Many types of constraints may be present on the project. The PMBOK® talks about four:
    - Organizational structure
    - Union agreements
    - Preferences of the project team
    - Staff assignments.

- **Arbitration** – The hearing and resolution of a dispute performed by a neutral party.

- **Perquisites** (perks) – Parking spaces, corner offices, executive dining.

- **Fringe Benefits** – Education, benefits, insurance, profit sharing.

- **Expectancy Theory** – Employees who believe that their efforts will lead to effective performance and who expect to be rewarded for their accomplishments stay productive as rewards meet their expectations.

- **Halo Effect** – The tendency to rate high or low on *all* factors due to the impression of a high or low rating on *some* specific factor. This can also mean, "You are a great programmer so therefore we will make you a project manager and also expect you to be great."

- **War Room** – The project team is located in one room. It makes the project more tangible and creates a project identity for the project team and management in a matrix organization.

SAMPLE QUESTIONS
Human Resource Management

	3rd Time	2nd Time	1st Time

1) Which of the following is not a form of power derived from the project manager's position:
   A. Formal
   B. Reward
   C. Penalty
   D. Expert

2) The peak point of Maslow's hierarchy of needs is called:
   A. Physiological satisfaction
   B. Attainment of survival
   C. The need for association
   D. None of the above

3) The Halo effect is important to know because there is a tendency to:
   A. Promote from within
   B. Hire the best
   C. Move people into project management because they are good in their technical field
   D. Move people into project management because they have had project management training

4) An obstacle to team building in a matrix organization is:
   A. Team organization is technically focused
   B. Team members are borrowed resources and can be hard to motivate
   C. Teams are too centralized
   D. Teams are too large to handle

5) Which of the following is not a typical concern of matrixed team members?
   A. Wondering who will handle their evaluations
   B. Serving multiple bosses
   C. Developing commitment
   D. Computing fringe benefits when working on multiple projects

6) Which of the following conflict resolution techniques will generate the most lasting solution?
   A. Forcing
   B. Smoothing
   C. Compromise
   D. Problem solving

© May 2000 (Registered) Rita Mulcahy, PMP at RMC – Project Management
PHONE: (612) 929-7539, EMAIL: rita@rmcproject.com, WEB: rmcproject.com

7) Complex projects involving cross-disciplinary efforts are best managed by a ___ organization.

    A.   Projectized
    B.   Functional
    C.   Line
    D.   Matrix

8) The most common causes of conflict on a project are?

    A.   Schedules, project priorities, personalities
    B.   Schedules, project priorities, resources
    C.   Schedules, project priorities, cost
    D.   Schedules, project priorities, management

9) "Why can't we solve this problem by all sides giving in a little?" This is an example of what type of conflict resolution technique?

    A.   Problem solving
    B.   Forcing
    C.   Withdrawal
    D.   Compromising

10) What does a responsibility Gantt chart show that a responsibility matrix does not?

    A.   Time
    B.   Tasks
    C.   Interrelationships
    D.   Who is in charge of each task

ANSWERS
1 D
2 D
3 C
4 B
5 D
6 D
7 D
8 B
9 D
10 A

Chapter 9

Communication Management
(PMBOK® Chapter 10)

Communication questions are generally very easy. However, many of my students comment that the number of communication questions on the exam surprises them. Remember, although there may be only 10 questions from the material in this chapter on the exam, there are many other communication questions addressed in other parts of the book. For example, a WBS is a communication tool (see the Scope chapter) and actions planned to mitigate risks should be communicated (in the Risk chapter.)

Lack of communication is high on most project manager's list of common project problems. It is therefore important that a project manager has some background in proper communication techniques so that he/she can improve his/her own communications. Read and understand the following but note that none of the lists and bullet points, except the communication model, need to be memorized.

HOT TOPICS include:
- Communication methods
  - Formal
  - Informal
  - Written
  - Verbal
- Performance reporting
- Administrative closure
- Communication blockers
- Communication planning
- Communication Management Plan
- Communication model
  - Nonverbal
  - Paralingual
  - Active listening
  - Effective listening
  - Feedback
- Control of communication
- Communication channels

COMMUNICATION PLANNING (page 105): Communication planning involves "determining the information and communication needs of the stakeholders." This is, once again, a very pro-active approach. PMI® is saying that this requires a conscious plan, and therefore, project managers must think about this and put a formal written plan together.

Communications can take place many ways including face-to-face, by telephone, fax, email, or meetings. It is important to know that 90% of the project manager's time is spent communicating.

COMMUNICATION MANAGEMENT PLAN (page 106): This plan is created by the project manager and becomes part of the project plan. It may include:
- What information needs to be collected and when
- Who will receive the information
- Methods used to gather and store information
- Who may talk to whom
- Reporting relationships
- Schedule for distribution of each type of communication

ADMINISTRATIVE CLOSURE (page 109): At the end of each project results must be verified and documented, formal acceptance received, and project records collected. You should know the inputs and outputs listed in the PMBOK and also how such closure differs from contract closeout (page 133) in procurement. Spend some time on this, and also with the listing on page 19. There can be many questions on this topic!

COMMUNICATION MODEL (pages 23 and 107): Many of my students think that understanding the communication model is trivial. However, they begin to realize its importance when they note how many communications problems project managers have on projects. If communication is not working, one solution is to review what and how you are communicating – look at the communication model.

The communication model looks like a circle with three parts: the sender, the message, and the receiver. Each message is encoded by the sender and decoded by the receiver based on the receiver's education, experience, language, and culture. PMI® advocates that the sender encode a message carefully, determine the communication method (listed below) to use to send it, and confirm that the message is understood. The receiver should decode the message carefully and confirm that the message is understood.

The following terms sometimes show up on the exam:

- **NONVERBAL** – about 55% of all communication is non-verbal (e.g., based on physical mannerisms).
- **PARALINGUAL** – means the pitch and tone of your voice. This also helps to convey a message.
- **ACTIVE LISTENING** – The receiver confirms that she is listening, confirms agreement, and asks for clarification.
- **EFFECTIVE LISTENING** – Watching the speaker to pick up physical gestures and facial expressions, thinking about what you want to say before responding, asking questions, repeating, and providing feedback.
- **FEEDBACK** – "Do you understand what I have explained," usually done by the sender.

COMMUNICATION METHODS (page 107): On the "old exam" this topic consisted of a majority of the communication questions. The "new" exam should have less communication questions but a majority of them should still be about communication methods. You must be able to pick the form of communication that is best for a situation. These questions should be very easy if you know the following chart:

Communication Method	When Used
Formal written	Complex problems, Project Plans, Charter, communicating over long distances
Formal verbal	Presentations, speeches
Informal written	Memos, e-mail, notes
Informal verbal	Meetings, conversations

CONTROL OF COMMUNICATION: The exam may also ask:
- Can the project manager control all communication? The answer is no! That would be impossible.
- Should the project manager try to control communications? Yes, otherwise changes, miscommunications, unclear directions, and scope creep can occur.
- What percent of the project manager's time is spent communicating? About 90%.

COMMUNICATION BLOCKERS: Phrases such as "what is your game plan," "getting down to the nitty-gritty," or even "zero in on problems" can cause miscommunication with people from other cultures. So can such comment as "What a bad idea!" The exam has often had one or two questions that ask "What can get in the way of communications?" The answer may include:

- Noise
- Distance
- Improper en-coding of messages
- Saying "that is a bad idea"
- Hostility
- Language
- Culture

PERFORMANCE REPORTING (pages 107-109): Reports should provide the kinds of information and the level of detail required by various stakeholders. Reports are communication tools and take different forms, including:

- STATUS REPORT – Describing where the project now stands

- PROGRESS REPORT – Describing what has been accomplished

- TREND REPORT – Examining project results over time to see if performance is improving or deteriorating

- FORECASTING REPORT – Predicting future project status and performance

- VARIANCE REPORT – Comparing actual results to planned

- EARNED VALUE – Integrating scope, cost, and schedule measures to assess project performance. This report makes use of the terms described under cost (e.g., BCWS, BCWP, ACWP, etc).

COMMUNICATION CHANNELS: Communications grow at greater than a linear rate and are represented by the following formula: N (N-1)/2 where N equals the number of people. You should know this formula. The intent is for the project manager to realize that communication is complex and needs to be managed but cannot be controlled.

> POINTER: Anytime you see a formula containing the letter "N," even if it looks slightly different than the formula above, that formula represents communication channels.

> Sample question: *If a team of four people adds one more person to the team, how many more channels of communication are there?*

> Answer: *Four more channels of communication.* There were six communications channels. Using the formula above, there are now ten. The question asks how many MORE so the answer is 10 – 6, or four.

SAMPLE QUESTIONS
Communications Management

	3rd Time	2nd Time	1st Time

1) Extensive use of ___ communication is most likely to aid in solving complex problems.
   A. Verbal
   B. Written
   C. Formal
   D. A management information system

2) The WBS can be an effective aid for ___ communication:
   A. Internal within the project team
   B. Internal within the organization
   C. External with the customer
   D. A, B and C

3) Conflict resolution techniques that may be used on a project include:
   A. Confronting, smoothing, forcing, and withdrawing
   B. Confronting, controlling, directing, forcing
   C. Confronting, compromising, controlling, organizing
   D. Confronting, smoothing, forcing, and controlling

4) The existence of communication barriers is likely to cause:
   A. The project to be on time
   B. Trust level to be enhanced
   C. Conflict to occur
   D. Senior management to be pleased

5) Communication is often enhanced when the sender ___ the receiver.
   A. Speaks up to
   B. Uses more physical movements
   C. Talks slowly to
   D. Shows concern for the perspective of

6) Formal, written correspondence with the customer is required when:
   A. Defects are detected
   B. The customer requests additional work not covered under contract
   C. The project has a schedule slippage
   D. The project has cost overruns

7) The project has a problem with personnel performance. This is best handled through:
   A. Formal written communication
   B. Formal verbal communication
   C. Informal written communication
   D. Informal verbal communication

8) Communication under a contract should tend toward:
   A. Formal written communication
   B. Formal verbal communication
   C. Informal written communication
   D. Informal verbal communication

9) The project status report is an example of which form of communication?
   A. Formal written communication
   B. Formal verbal communication
   C. Informal written communication
   D. Informal verbal communication

10) When a project manager is engaged in negotiations, non-verbal communication skills are of:
   A. Little importance
   B. Major importance
   C. Important only when cost and schedule objectives are involved
   D. Important only when dealing with other cultures

11) You have just been assigned project manager for a large telecommunications project. This one-year project is about halfway done, and it involves three different vendors and thirty people on the project team. You would like to see the communications requirements for the project and what technology is being used to aid in project communications. What should you refer to?
   A. The project plan
   B. The information distribution plan
   C. The Gantt chart
   D. The communications management plan

12) Contract close-out is similar to administrative closure in that they both involve:
   A. Product verification
   B. Kick off meetings
   C. Quality assurance activities
   D. Creation of the scope verification plan

13) An output of administrative closure is:
   A. The creation of project archives
   B. The creation of a project charter
   C. The creation of a risk analysis plan
   D. The creation of a project plan

ANSWERS:
1 B
2 D
3 A
4 C
5 D
6 B
7 D
8 A
9 A
10 B
11 D
12 A
13 A

Chapter 10

Risk Management
(PMBOK® Chapter 11)

This is one of the three hardest topics (along with quality and cost) on the exam primarily because:
- So few people have any education in risk management.
- A lot of potential test material exists.
- Questions frequently ask, "what do you do in this type of situation."
- You must know the process of risk management.
- The questions can be asked many ways.

HOT TOPICS in order of importance:
- Risk management process
- Definition of risk
- Expected monetary value
- Risk Identification
- Risk Quantification
- Risk Response Development
- Risk Response Control
- Qualification
- Inputs to risk management
- Outputs from risk quantification
- Risk Management Plan
- Alternative strategies
  - Avoidance
  - Mitigation
  - Acceptance
  - Deflection
- Monte Carlo simulation
- Contingency plans
- Workarounds
- Reserves
- Contracting
- Sources of risk
- Types of risk
- Definition of risk management
- Risk symptoms
- Risk tolerances
- Uncertainty
- Decision trees
- Risk averse
- Risk factors
- Insurance

It is important to understand that project risks can be substantially decreased. Some studies quote a 90% decrease in project problems through the use of risk management. Risk management is actually a very proactive task. Through the process of risk management we change from the project being in control of the project manager to the project manager being in control of the project.

You do not have to be risk management experts to pass risk questions on the exam nor will this chapter make you an expert. It will provide the overview necessary for the exam but you should realize that there are more tools and techniques to real world risk management.

Although the exam does not require memorization of PMBOK® definitions, I have found that knowing some definitions in risk can help you find answers to exam questions. You should know all the definitions presented but you must know the process of risk management and what happens when in the process. This chapter is full of important descriptions so read every word carefully!

DEFINITION OF A RISK OR RISK EVENT: "A discrete occurrence that may affect the project for good or bad." NOTE: Do not forget that there can be good risks!

DEFINITION OF UNCERTAINTY: "An uncommon state of nature, characterized by the absence of any information related to a desired outcome."

DEFINITION OF RISK MANAGEMENT (page 111): "The processes involved with identifying, analyzing and responding to risk. It includes maximizing the results of positive events and minimizing the consequences of adverse events."

RISK AVERSE: Someone who does not want to take risks.

INPUTS TO RISK MANAGEMENT or what do you need before you begin the risk management process (page 113):
- All project background information
- Historical records
- Past Lessons Learned
- Project charter
- Scope Statement
- Scope of work
- WBS
- Network diagram
- Cost and time estimates
- Staffing plan

RISK MANAGEMENT PROCESS (page 111): This is an important topic. You must know what happens when, how the risk management process works on a real project, and how it relates to the project life cycle. The risk management process contains four steps:

1. RISK IDENTIFICATION
2. RISK QUANTIFICATION
3. RISK RESPONSE DEVELOPMENT
4. RISK RESPONSE CONTROL

STEP 1: RISK IDENTIFICATION – Defined as "determining which risks are likely to affect the project and documenting the characteristics of each risk." Smart project managers begin looking for risks as soon as a project is first discussed. However, the major risk identification effort occurs during Planning. This step cannot be completed until a WBS has been created and the project team knows "what is the project." Because risk identification can occur during the Initiation and Planning phases, the exam has often said that risk identification happens at the *onset* of the project.

Risks may be identified at the beginning of the project, during each project phase, and before approval of a major scope change. Risks may also be identified during all phases of the project including Initiation, Planning, Execution, Control, and Closeout. In other words, although the major risk identification effort occurs at the onset of the project, risks should continue to be identified throughout the project.

TYPES OF RISK – Risks can be classified under two main types:
1. Business – Risk of a gain or loss
2. Pure (Insurable) Risk – Only a risk of loss (e.g., fire, theft, personal injury)

SOURCES OF RISK – A prior version of the PMBOK® included information about various sources of risk in terms of the following. The concept still shows up on the exam from time to time. Risks can come from:

- EXTERNAL – Regulatory, environmental, government, market shifts
- INTERNAL – Schedule, cost, unforeseen conditions, scope changes, inexperience, poor planning, people, staffing, materials, equipment
- TECHNICAL – Changes in technology
- UNFORESEEABLE – Only a small portion of risks (some say about 10%) are actually unforeseeable.

The exam most always refers to the following as sources of risk (these are the triple constraints or what the project manager must juggle when managing the project):

- Schedule
- Cost
- Quality
- Performance or scope of work

RISK FACTORS (page 114) – When looking at risk one should look at:

- The probability that it will occur (what)
- The range of possible outcomes (impact or amount at stake)
- Expected timing (when) the project life cycle
- Anticipated frequency of risk events from that source (how often)

RISK SYMPTOMS (TRIGGERS page 114) – A project manager should determine what are the early warning signs (indirect manifestations of actual risk events) for each risk on a project so that they will know when to take action.

RISK TOLERANCES (page 115) – You should have an understanding of the amount of risk that is acceptable (tolerance level.) For example, "a risk that effects our reputation will not be tolerated," or " a risk of a two-week delay is okay, but nothing more." Tolerance levels are discovered in step 1 and used in step 2 to evaluate risks.

STEP 2: RISK QUANTIFICATION – "Assessing the risks and risk interactions to assess the range of possible project outcomes. It is primarily concerned with determining which risk events warrant a response."

Risk Quantification involves determining the following for each risk. *NOTE: The PMBOK® is not clear where the following steps belong, in Identification or Quantification. Common business practice around the world is to include these items in Quantification.*

- Probability
- Amount at stake (or impact)
- Developing a ranking of risks

Two methods can be used to determine probability and amount at stake:

QUALITATIVE – taking an educated guess (e.g., High, Medium, Low or 1 to 10)
QUANTITATIVE – estimating by calculation (e.g., US $20,000 or 3-week delay)

PMI® suggests that the quantitative method (also referred to as quantification) is the preferable method because it is less subjective and is a better approximation of actual probabilities and impacts but both are acceptable.

NOTE: PMI® refers to steps 1 and 2 combined as *risk assessment*. Be careful if you see this word on the exam

MONTE CARLO SIMULATION (page 117 and the chart on page 118) – As previously described, this simulation "performs" the project many times and uses the network diagram and PERT estimates to simulate the cost or schedule results of the project. I would like to add the following items to your knowledge of Monte Carlo relating to risk:

- It indicates the risk of the project and each task by providing a percent probability that each task will be on the Critical Path.
- It accounts for path convergence (page 118). Simply, where paths in a Network Diagram converge into one task, that task is riskier than looking at the task alone. The chart on PMBOK® page 118 gives a more complex explanation.

EXPECTED MONETARY VALUE (OR EXPECTED VALUE page 115) – The product of two numbers, probability and impact (or the amount at stake). This is the second most-tested topic after the process of risk management. The questions can ask, "What is the expected value of a task or of a series of task?" Expected value questions can also be asked in conjunction with decision trees noted in this chapter.

Exercise:

INSTRUCTIONS: Test yourself! Complete the following chart.

Task	Probability	Impact (Amount At Stake)	Expected Value
A	10%	US $20,000	
B	30%	US $45,000	
C	68%	US $18,000	

Answer:

I hope it makes you feel better that something on the exam is easy!

Task	Probability	Impact (Amount At Stake)	Expected Value
A	10%	US $20,000	US $2,000
B	30%	US $45,000	US $13,500
C	68%	US $18,000	US $12,240

Expected value has one very important advantage. It helps you define and prove what your reserve (contingency budget, management reserve, etc.) should be! To illustrate expected value and the calculation of a reserve, let's try a harder example.

Exercise:

INSTRUCTIONS: Test yourself! Assuming that these are all the risks for the project, calculate the amount of your budget reserve. You may use the worksheet provided below.

You are planning the manufacture of an existing product's modifications. Your analysis has come up with the following:

- 30% probability of a delay in the receipt of parts with a cost to the project of US $50,000.
- 20% probability that the parts will be US $10,000 cheaper than expected.
- 25% probability that two parts will not fit together when installed, resulting in an extra US $3,500.
- 30% probability that the manufacture may be simpler than expected, resulting in a savings of US $2,500.
- 5% probability of a design defect causing US $5,000 of rework.

130

Answer:

The answer is:

30% x US $50,000	Add US $15,000
20% x US $10,000	Subtract US $2,000
25% x US $3,500	Add US $875
30% x US $2,500	Subtract US $750
5% x US $5,000	Add US $250
TOTAL	US $13,375

DECISION TREES (page 117 and a picture on 119) – There can be up to three exam questions about decision trees. See the diagram in PMBOK® page 119. You should know the following:
- A decision tree takes into account future events in trying to make a decision today.
- It makes use of expected value (probability times impact) calculations and mutual exclusivity (previously explained)
- Be able to draw a simple one or to answer questions about one that is included in the exam.

The following exercise shows a picture of a decision tree. The box represents a decision to be made and the circles represent what can happen as a result of the decision.

Exercise:

INSTRUCTIONS: Based on the picture below, what is the expected value for the line X?

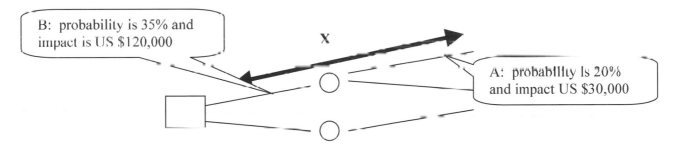

Answer:

The answer is US $48,000 as follows:

35% x US $120,000 = US $42,000
20% x US $30,000 = US $6,000
Total expected value is the summation of both calculations or US $48,000

OUTPUTS FROM RISK QUANTIFICATION (page 117) – When completed, risk quantification results in a prioritized list of risks and:

- Determination of top risks
- Opportunities to pursue
- Opportunities to ignore
- Threats to respond to
- Threats to ignore

STEP 3: RISK RESPONSE DEVELOPMENT (page 119-121) – This step involves figuring out "what are we going to do about it." This step involves finding ways to make the risk smaller or eliminate it entirely. You should note that all project risks cannot be eliminated. Risk response development involves the following activities:

ALTERNATIVE STRATEGIES – (Sometimes called risk mitigation strategies.) Changing the planned approach to completing the project. This may involve changes to the WBS, schedule, and budget. The choices to do this are listed on the exam as:

- **AVOIDANCE** - Eliminate the threat by eliminating the cause

- **MITIGATION** - Effect the probability or the impact of the risk

- **ACCEPTANCE** - Do nothing and say "If it happens, it happens"

- **DEFLECTION (TRANSFER, ALLOCATE)** – Make another party responsible for the risk through allocation, purchasing of insurance, or outsourcing the work

In each case communication of risks and strategies is necessary as part of the strategy.

NOTE: Deflection is not listed in the PMBOK® but often appears on the exam! The PMBOK® may have intended it to be part of mitigation.

OUTPUTS FROM RISK RESPONSE DEVELOPMENT include:

INSURANCE – A response to certain risks such as fire, property, or personnel injury insurance (e.g., pure risks) is to purchase insurance. Insurance exchanges an unknown risk for a known risk.

CONTRACTING – Hiring someone more experienced to do the work that is causing the risk to diminish the overall project risk. NOTE: You cannot remove all the specific risk from a project by contracting. If there is a risk of damage in transport for a project component, then hiring someone else to do the transportation will not make the move risk-free.

CONTINGENCY PLANNING (Planned responses) – Specific actions you will take if a risk event occurs.

RESERVES (CONTINGENCY) – Formulating the amount of time or cost that needs to be added to the project to account for risk. These are sometimes called management reserves (to account for "unknown unknowns") and contingency reserves (to account for "known unknowns"). PMI® recommends a minimum a total reserve of 10%.

RISK MANAGEMENT PLAN – A written document that documents the risks you identified and what you plan to do about it. The project manager should also record non-critical risks so that they can easily be revisited during the Execution Phase.

The exam often asks questions such as:

- *What do you do with non-critical risks? Answer: Document and revisit periodically.*
- *Would you select only one risk response strategy? Answer: No, you can choose a combination of choices.*
- *What risk management activities would you be doing during the Execution Phase of the project? Answer: Watching out for non-critical risks that become more important.*
- *What is the most important item to address in project team meetings? Answer: Risk.*
- *How would risks be addressed in project meetings? By asking, "What is the status of risks? Any new risks? Any change to the order of importance?"*

STEP 4: RISK RESPONSE CONTROL (pages 121- 122) – This step may include such activities as executing and updating the Risk Management Plan, re-planning, going through steps 1 through 3 when changes occur, and managing risks. It can also include executing the following:

WORKAROUNDS (page 121) – *Unplanned responses* to risks or dealing with risks that you could not or did not anticipate.

CONTINGENCY PLANS (page 120) – *Planned responses* to risks or putting in place the contingency plans set up during risk response development.

One of the interesting questions on the exam has been:

Which are more frequent, contingency plans or workarounds?

Most project managers will say workarounds because that has been the project manager's experience. In fact with proper risk management workarounds become less frequent than contingency plans.

EXTRAS:
Keep in mind that many people do not have training in risk management and yet risk questions on the exam require you to have some experience in performing risk management in the workplace. The following is a synopsis of my presentation "Common Stumbling Blocks in Risk Management" that I have presented around the world. It will help improve your real world experience in risk management.

Common Stumbling Blocks in Risk Management:

1. Risk identification is completed without knowing enough about the project. (See Inputs to Risk Management.)

2. Project risk is evaluated using only questionnaire, interview or Monte Carlo techniques and thus does not provide a detailed, per task analysis of risk.

3. Risk identification ends too soon resulting in a brief list (20 risks) rather than an extensive list (hundreds of risks) of risks.

4. Steps 1 and 2 of risk management are blended resulting in risks that are evaluated or judged when they come to light. This decreases the number of total risks identified and causes people to stop participating in risk identification.

5. The risks identified are general rather than specific (e.g., "communication" rather than "poor communication of customers' needs regarding installation of system XXX caused two weeks of rework")

6. Whole categories of risks are missed such as technology, cultural or marketplace.

7. Only one method is used to identify risk rather than a combination of methods. A combination helps ensure that more risks are identified.

8. The first risk response strategy identified is selected without looking at other options and finding the best option or combination of options.

9. Risks are not given enough attention during the project Execution phase.

SAMPLE QUESTIONS
Risk Management

	3rd Time	2nd Time	1st Time

1) Which of the following is not a factor in the assessment of project risk?
   A. Risk event
   B. Risk probability
   C. Amount at stake
   D. Insurance premiums

2) If a project has a 60% chance of a US $100,000 profit and a 40% chance of a US $100,000 loss, the expected monetary value for the project is:
   A. US $100,000 profit
   B. US $60,000 loss
   C. US $20,000 profit
   D. US $40,000 loss

3) "An uncommon state of nature, characterized by the absence of any information related to a desired outcome," is a common definition for:
   A. Certainty
   B. The amount at stake
   C. Uncertainty
   D. Risk aversion

4) Assuming that the ends of a range of estimates are $\pm$ 3 sigma from the mean, which of the following range estimates involves the least risk?
   A. 30 days, plus or minus 5 days
   B. 22 - 30 days
   C. Optimistic – 26 days, most likely = 30 days, pessimistic – 33 days
   D. A and B are equivalent and are both less risky than C

5) Which of the following risk events is most likely to interfere with attainment of the project's schedule objective?
   A. Delays in obtaining required approvals
   B. Substantial increases in the cost of purchased materials
   C. Contract disputes that generate claims for increased payments
   D. Slippage of the planned post-implementation review meeting

6) If a risk has a 20% chance of happening in any given month, and if the project is expected to last five months, the probability that this risk event will occur during the last month of the project is:
   A. 20 %
   B. 40%
   C. 60%
   D. 100%

7) If a risk event has a 90% chance of occurring, and the impact will be US $10,000, what does US $9,000 represent?

    A.   Risk value
    B.   Present value
    C.   Expected value
    D.   Contingency budget

8) Risks will be identified during which phase of project management life cycle?

    A.   Initiation
    B.   Planning
    C.   Execution
    D.   All phases

9) What should be done with non-critical risks?

    A.   Ignore them, they are not critical enough to include in risk response development
    B.   Document them and revisit during project execution
    C.   Ignore them, they are already taken care of in your contingency plans
    D.   Document them so that they can be given to the customer

10) Which of the following is not an input to the risk management process?

    A.   Historical records
    B.   Lessons learned
    C.   WBS
    D.   Project status reports

11) During project execution a team member identifies a risk that is not in the risk management plan, you should:

    A.   Analyze the risk
    B.   Ignore the risk because you already performed a detailed analysis
    C.   Ignore the risk because risks were identified during planning
    D.   Tell the customer about the risk

12) During execution a major problem occurs that you did not include in your risk management plan, you should:

    A.   Create a work around
    B.   Have a meeting
    C.   Tell the customer
    D.   Tell management

13) Risk tolerances are determined to:

    A.   Help the team rank the project risks
    B.   Help the project manager estimate the project
    C.   Help the team schedule the project
    D.   Help management know how other managers will act on the project

14) Which of the following is not a common result of risk management?
   A.   Contract terms and conditions are created
   B.   The project plan is changed
   C.   The communication plan is changed
   D.   The project charter is changed

15) Purchasing insurance is an example of:
   A.   Risk initiation
   B.   Risk deflection
   C.   Risk acceptance
   D.   Risk avoidance

16) You are finding it difficult to evaluate the exact cost impact of risks, you should:
   A.   Evaluate them on a quantitative basis
   B.   Evaluate them on a numerical basis
   C.   Evaluate them on a qualitative basis
   D.   Do not evaluate them at all

17) The customer requests a change to the project that would increase the project risk. Which of the following would you do before all the others?
   A.   Include the expected value of the risk in the changed cost estimate
   B.   Talk to the customer about the impact of the change
   C.   Analyze the impacts of the change with the team
   D.   Change the risk management plan

18) An output from risk response development is:
   A.   Risk management plan
   B.   Risks identified
   C.   Control plan
   D.   Impacts identified

19) Workarounds are determined during which step of risk management?
   A.   Risk Identification
   B.   Risk Quantification
   C.   Risk Response Development
   D.   Risk Response Control

20) A determination to transfer a risk may be made during which step of risk management?
   A.   Risk Identification
   B.   Risk Quantification
   C.   Risk Response Development
   D.   Risk Response Control

© May 2000 (Registered) Rita Mulcahy, PMP at RMC – Project Management
PHONE: (612) 929-7539, EMAIL: rita@rmcproject.com, WEB: rmcproject.com

ANSWERS
1 D
2 C
3 C
4 C
5 A
6 A
7 C
8 D
9 B
10 D
11 A
12 A
13 A
14 D
15 B
16 C
17 C
18 A
19 D
20 C

Chapter 11

Procurement Management

(PMBOK® Chapter 12)

HOT TOPICS in order of importance:

- Procurement process
- Contract type selection
  - CR
  - CPFF
  - CPPC
  - CPIF
  - T&M
  - FP
  - FPIF
  - FPEPA
- Purchase Order
- Incentives
- Advantages / disadvantages of each contract form
- Contract close-out
- Contracting methods (Bid, RFP)
- Incentives
- Risk and contract type
- What forms a contract
- What makes up a contract
- Project manager's role
- Procurement documents
- Non-competitive procurement
- Types of SOW
- Make or buy
- Bidders conferences
- Conflict with contract administrator
- Contract change control system
- Evaluation criteria
- Special terms and conditions
- Standard contract terms and conditions
- Negotiation objectives/tactics
- Privity
- Qualified seller lists
- Advertising
- Benefits of centralized and decentralized contracting
- Definition of procurement management
- Contract interpretation
- Lessons learned

This topic can be very difficult if you have never worked with contracts or if you are unfamiliar with contracting in the US. Although difficult, it is only the fourth hardest topic after quality, cost, and risk.

Many procurement questions are process oriented (like risk management and the project life cycle) so you must know the steps of procurement management as outlined in the PMBOK® and what happens during each step. Be careful to read procurement questions carefully. The exam uses many different words for buyer and seller (e.g., owner, contractor, vendor, subcontractor). There are also a few definitions that will help you pick the correct answers to wordy questions.

NOTE: Most people are not aware of an essential piece of information that will make these questions easier. Unless it specifically states otherwise, the questions on procurement are from the buyer's perspective!

An overall tip for this chapter is to remember the following, especially if you get to a question that you do not know:

- A contract is a formal agreement.
- All requirements should be specifically stated in the contract.
- All contract requirements must be met.
- Changes must be in writing and formally controlled.
- The US government backs all contracts by providing a court system.

NOTE TO STUDENTS OUTSIDE THE USA – The exam has very few references to international contracts but you should be aware that government contracting specialists in the US wrote many of these questions. PMI®'s process for procurement management closely follows what is done in the US but is much more formal than how procurement is handled in many parts of the world. If you are not from the US, a key trick is to take a more formal approach to the procurement process when answering questions. Study this chapter carefully.

DEFINITION OF PROCUREMENT MANAGEMENT (page 123): "Includes the processes required to acquire goods and services from outside the performing organization."

WHAT FORMS A CONTRACT: Or, "What do you need in order to have a legal contract:"
1. An offer
2. Acceptance
3. Consideration – something of value, not necessarily money
4. Legal capacity – separate legal parties, competent parties
5. Legal purpose – you cannot have a contract for the sale of illegal goods

A contract, offer, or acceptance may be spoken or written though written is preferred.

WHAT MAKES UP A CONTRACT: Many project managers do not realize that "the contract" refers to legal and business terms and conditions as well as scope of work, marketing literature, drawings, charts, etc.

PROJECT MANAGER'S ROLE IN PROCUREMENT: As explained under risk management, the result of risk management is to have an understanding of what risks should or can be mitigated on the project. Although procurement, contracting, or legal professionals may handle the procurement, the project manager is the authority on project risks and can greatly assist in making the contract appropriate to the project. Contracts are in fact risk mitigation tools! Therefore, a contract should not be created before the project manager is assigned to the project. In addition, the project manager must be able to work within the procurement process in order to manage the project. For these two reasons and many others, project managers MUST understand contracts.

THE PROCUREMENT MANAGEMENT PROCESS (page 123): Procurement management is a step-by-step process. The exam should ask questions that require you to know the steps and what happens during each. Here is a trick to do so:

STEP	BUZZ WORDS TO REMEMBER
1. Procurement planning	Make or buy
2. Solicitation planning	RFP
3. Solicitation	Q & A
4. Source selection	Pick one
5. Contract administration	Admin
6. Contract closeout	Finish

Steps to Procurement Management

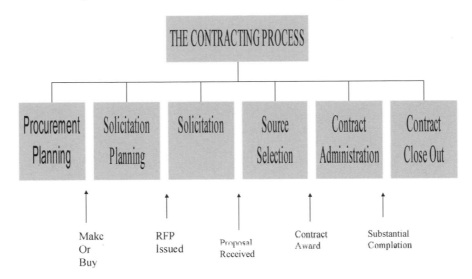

STEP 1: PROCUREMENT PLANNING (pages 125 - 127): The buzz word for this step is "MAKE OR BUY" and consists of "identifying which project needs can best be met by procuring goods or services outside the project organization." Two main issues to be addressed are:

> **MAKE OR BUY** (page 126) – The project can make all it needs, buy all it needs or any range in between. (As simple as this sounds it has been a question on the exam!) PMI® advocates that the actual out-of-pocket costs to purchase the product as well as the indirect cost of managing the procurement be considered in any "make or buy" decision. The cost savings to purchase may be outweighed by the cost of managing the procurement.
>
> One of the main reasons to buy is to decrease risk (cost, schedule, and performance or scope of work). It is better to "make" if:
>
> - You have an idle plant or workforce
> - You want to retain control
> - The work involves proprietary information or procedures.
>
> Sometimes the make or buy analysis involves a buy or lease question such as:
> *You are trying to decide whether to lease or buy some item for your project. The daily lease cost is $120. To purchase the item the investment cost is $1000 and the daily cost is $20. How long will it take for the lease cost to be the same as the purchase cost?*
>
> *ANSWER: Let D equal the number of days when the purchase and lease costs are equal*
> $$120D = $1,000 + $20D$$
> $$120D - $20D = $1,000$$
> $$100D = $1,000$$
> *D= $10 or the lease cost will be the same as the purchase cost after 10 days. If you think you will need the item for more than 10 days you should consider purchasing it to reduce total costs.*

CONTRACT TYPE SELECTION (page 126) – This is an important topic! You must understand all the following contract types and be able to tell the difference. The objective of contract type selection is to have reasonable distribution of risk between the buyer and seller and the greatest incentive for the seller's efficient and economical performance.

The following factors may influence the type of contract selected:
- How well-defined the scope of work is or can be
- The amount or frequency of changes expected after the project starts
- The amount of effort and expertise the buyer can devote to managing the seller
- Industry standards of type of contract used

There are generally three types for contracts:
1. CR – Cost reimbursable
2. FP – Fixed price
3. T&M – Time and material

COST REIMBURSABLE (CR) – The seller's costs are reimbursed but the buyer bears the highest risk of all contract forms that the costs will increase – e.g. cost risk. Common forms of cost reimbursable contracts include:

CPFF – Cost Plus Fixed Fee. This is the most common form of cost reimbursable contracts. In this form of contract, the buyer will pay all costs, but the fee (or profit) will be fixed at a specific dollar amount. This helps to keep the seller's cost in line because a cost overrun will not generate any additional fee or profit.

> EXAMPLE: Contract = Cost plus a fee of $100,000.

CPPC – Cost Plus Percentage of Costs. This is an illegal form of contract for the US government and is bad for buyers everywhere. Can you guess why?

This type of cost reimbursable contract requires the buyer to pay for all costs plus a percent of costs as a fee. Sellers are not motivated to control costs because the seller will get paid profit on every cost without limit.

> EXAMPLE: Contract = Cost plus 10% of costs as fee.

CPIF – Cost Plus Incentive Fee. This type of cost reimbursable contract pays all costs and an agreed upon fee, plus a bonus for beating the incentive. See more on incentive clauses at the end of this topic.

> EXAMPLE: Contract = Cost plus a fee of $100,000. For every month the project is completed sooner than agreed upon, seller will receive an additional $10,000.

TIME AND MATERIAL (T&M) – or Unit Price – Usually used for small dollar amounts. This form of contract is priced on a per hour or per item basis and has elements of a fixed price contract (in the price per hours) and a cost reimbursable contract (in the material costs). In this form the buyer has a medium amount of cost risk, as compared to CR and FP, because the contract is usually for small dollar amounts

> EXAMPLE: Contract = $100 per hour plus materials at cost or $5 per linear foot of wood.

FIXED PRICE (FP) (sometimes called lump sum or firm fixed price) – This is the most common form of contract in the world. In this form of contract one price is agreed upon for all the work. In this form, the buyer has the least cost risk, the risk of costs going higher is born by the seller.

> EXAMPLE: Contract = $1,100,000.

FPIF – There are also incentive for fixed price contracts. This is called **Fixed Price Incentive Fee**. The incentive is the same as CPIF above.

> EXAMPLE: Contract = $1,100,000. For every month you finish the project early, you will receive $10,000.

FPEPA – Fixed Price Economic Price Adjustment. Sometimes a fixed price contract will allow for price increases if the contract is for multiple years.

> EXAMPLE: Contract = $1,100,000 but a price increase will be allowed in year 2 based on the US Consumer Price Increase report for year 1. Or the contract price is $1,100,000 but a price increase will be allowed in year 2 to account for increases in specific material costs.

PURCHASE ORDER – A form of contract that is unilateral (signed by one party) instead of bilateral (signed by both parties). It is usually used for simple commodity procurements.

> EXAMPLE: Contract to purchase 30 linear meters of wood at US $9 per meter.

INCENTIVES – allows an incentive (or bonus) on top of the agreed upon price for beating cost, time, performance, scope of work, or quality. *An incentive helps bring the seller's objectives in line with the buyer's.* With an incentive both buyer and seller work toward the same objective, for instance, completing the project on time. You should have some experience calculating the revised fee and total costs associated with this type of contract (see the next exercise). Such questions occasionally appear on the exam.

Exercise: Incentive Fee Calculations

There is only a small probability that you will be asked to calculate incentives. Therefore do not spend too much time on this! <u>INSTRUCTIONS</u>: Calculate both the fee <u>and</u> the final price.

In the first example, the cost is estimated at US $210,000 and the fee at US $25,000. If the seller beats that cost (an incentive), they will share the savings of 80% to the buyer and 20% to the seller. Remember the sharing ratio is always buyer/seller! Here all prices are in US $.

Cost Plus Incentive Fee Calculation

Target cost	$ 210,000
Target fee	$ 25,000
Target price	$ 235,000
Sharing ratio	80/20
Actual cost	$ 200,000

Fee	
Final price	

Fixed Price Plus Incentive Fee Calculation, #1

Target cost	$ 150,000
Target fee	$ 30,000
Target price	$ 180,000
Sharing ratio	60/40
Ceiling price	$ 200,000
Actual cost	$ 210,000

Fee	
Final price	

Fixed Price Plus Incentive Fee Calculation #2

Target cost	$ 9,000,000
Target fee	$ 850,000
Target price	$ 9,850,000
Sharing ratio	70/30
Ceiling price	$ 12,500,000
Actual cost	$ 8,000,000

Fee	
Final price	

Answers: Incentive Fee Calculations

Note: Remember, you many have to calculate both the fee <u>and</u> the final price for the exam!

Cost Plus Incentive Fee Calculation

Target cost	$ 210,000
Target fee	$ 25,000
Target price	$ 235,000
Sharing ratio	80/20
Actual cost	$ 200,000

Fee	• $210,000 – $200,000 = $10,000 x 20% = $2,000 • $25,000 target fee + $2,000 = $27,000 fee
Final price	$200,000 + $27000 = $227,000

Fixed Price Plus Incentive Fee Calculation #1

Target cost	$ 150,000
Target fee	$ 30,000
Target price	$ 180,000
Sharing ratio	60/40
Ceiling price	$ 200,000
Actual cost	$ 210,000

Fee	• $150,000 - $210,000 = ($60,000) an overage • ($60,000) x 40% = ($24,000) • $30,000 + ($24,000) = $6,000
Final price	• $210,000 + $6,000 = $216,000 • However, this is above the ceiling price of $200,000. • So the final price is $200,000.

Fixed Price Plus Incentive Fee Calculation #2

Target cost	$ 9,000,000
Target fee	$ 850,000
Target price	$ 9,850,000
Sharing ratio	70/30
Ceiling price	$ 12,500,000
Actual cost	$ 8,000,000

Fee	• $9,000,000 - $8,000,000 = $1,000,000 X 30% = $300,000 • ORIGINAL FEE OF $850,000 + $300,000 = $1,150,000
Final price	$8,000,000 + $1,150,000 FEE = $9,150,000 FINAL PRICE

ADVANTAGES AND DISADVANTAGES OF EACH CONTRACT FORM: This exercise helps test if you really understand the different forms of contracts.

Exercise:

<u>INSTRUCTIONS</u>: In the chart below, write the advantages and disadvantages of each form of contract for the BUYER. Since CPFF is the most common form of cost reimbursable contract, we will use CPFF here.

CPFF	T&M	FP
Advantages	**Advantages**	**Advantages**
Disadvantages	**Disadvantages**	**Disadvantages**

Answer: I could list many more advantages and disadvantages. Did you identify these?   Do you understand them?

CPFF	T&M	FP
Advantages	**Advantages**	**Advantages**
Lower cost than fixed price	Quick	Less work for buyer to manage
Less work to write the Scope of Work	Brief contract	Seller has a strong incentive to control costs
Cheaper than fixed price because the seller does not have to add as much for risk	Good choice when you are hiring "bodies" or people to augment your staff	Companies have experience with this form
		Buyer knows the total price

Disadvantages	Disadvantages	Disadvantages
Requires auditing	Profit is in every hour billed	Seller may charge extra on change orders
More work to manage	Seller has no incentive to control costs	Seller may try to get out of some of the scope of work if they begin to loose money
Seller has only a moderate incentive to control costs	Appropriate only for small projects	More work for buyer to write the Scope of Work
The total price is unknown		More expensive than CR because of additions seller adds for risk

RISK AND CONTRACT TYPE: The exam may ask questions that connect risk with the different forms of contracts. For example:

Who has the risk in a cost reimbursable contract, buyer or seller?
Answer – Buyer! If the costs increase the buyer pays the added costs.

Who has the cost risk in a fixed price contract, buyer or seller?
Answer – Seller! If costs increase the seller pays the costs and makes less profit.

TYPES OF SCOPE OF WORK (SOW page 127): A scope of work is written to describe what work is to be completed under the contract. Many types of scope of work exist. The choice among them should depend on the nature of the work and the type of industry.

- Performance – Conveys what the final product should be able to accomplish rather than how it should be built or what its design characteristics should be.

- Functional or detailed – Conveys the end purpose or results rather than specific procedures, etc. It is to be used in the performance of the work and may also include a statement of the minimum essential characteristics of the product.

- Design – Conveys precisely how the work is to be done.

Components of a Scope of Work include drawings, specifications, technical and descriptive wording, etc. No matter what it contains, you should realize that the scope of work becomes part of the contract.

Exercise:

INSTRUCTIONS: Complete the following to describe how detailed the scope of work must be for each type of contract.

- For a CR contract?

_____

_____

- For a T&M contract?

_____

_____

- For a FP contract?

_____

_____

Answer:

How will the contract type effect your Scope of Work?

- For a CR contract?

  In this case, the Scope of Work can describe only the performance or requirements because we are buying the expertise of "how to do the work." We may not be able to say exactly what to do or when. This form of scope of work is appropriate for Information Services, Information Technology, high tech, and "never been done before" type projects.

- For a T&M contract?

  The Scope of Work may be a brief description of functional, performance or design requirements. This form is appropriate for work to be completed over a short period of time or small dollar volumes, such as hiring a plumber or electrician.

- For a FP contract?

  The Scope of Work must be extraordinarily complete because we are buying "do it," not "how to do it." Often this Scope of Work is written by an outside company such as a design firm that is hired to design a building and to create the design that will be used in the scope of work. This form is appropriate when a complete scope of work can be written, (e.g., in the construction industry).

Be careful, this is a general approach. There are many reasons to handle contracts differently. However, using an inappropriate contract form can result in project failure, increased risk and conflict.

STEP 2: SOLICITATION PLANNING (page 127 – 129): The buzzword for this step is "RFP," and primarily consists of putting together the procurement documents.

PROCUREMENT DOCUMENTS (bid documents) are the documents put together by the buyer to tell the seller their needs. These documents may consist of the following parts:

- Information for sellers
  - Background information
  - Procedures for replying
  - Guidelines for preparation of the proposal
  - Evaluation criteria (described later)
  - Pricing forms
- Scope of work
- Proposed terms and conditions of the contract

Note that the contract is included in the procurement (BID) documents. Can you answer why? The terms and conditions of the contract are the work that needs to be done and the costs associated with them. The seller must know what ALL the work is to adequately understand and price the project.

Well-designed procurement (bid) documents can have the following effects on the project:
- Easier comparison of sellers' responses
- More complete proposals
- More accurate pricing
- Decrease in the amount of changes to the project

You should know that sellers can make suggestions for changes in the procurement documents including the scope of work and the project plan.

Procurement documents may take the following form:
- **REQUEST FOR PROPOSAL (RFP)** – (sometimes called request for tender) Requests a detailed proposal on how the work will be accomplished, who will do it, etc.
- **INVITATION FOR BID (IFB, or Request for Bid, RFB)** – Requests one price to do all the work.
- **REQUEST FOR QUOTATION (RFQ)** – Requests a price quote per item, hour, etc.

The choice of which type of procurement document to use depends on the form of scope of work and contract type selected.

Exercise:

INSTRUCTIONS: Test yourself! In the space provided below, write the contract type (FP, CR, T&M) that applies next to the procurement document, and the type of Scope of Work (Performance, Functional, or Design) to be used.

Procurement Documents	Contract Type	Scope Of Work
Request for Proposal (RFP)		
Invitation for Bid (IFB)		
Request for Quotation (RFQ)		

Answer:

This is a general approach to promote understanding. In the world of contracts, an infinite variety of procurement documents and contract types exist. The exam keeps things simple.

Procurement Documents	Contract Type	Scope Of Work
Request for Proposal (RFP)	CR	Performance or Functional
Invitation for Bid (IFB)	FP	Design
Request for Quotation (RFQ)	T&M	ANY

TERMS AND CONDITIONS: The following are *some of the standard terms and conditions in a contract*. You should be generally familiar with these definitions.

- Acceptance – How will you specifically know if the work is acceptable?
- Agent – Who is an authorized representative of each party?
- Authority – Who has the power to do what?
- Breach – When a part of the contract is not performed (remember, the contract consists of the Scope of Work and legal terms).
- Changes – How will they be made, what forms used, timeframe for notice and turnaround?
- Confidentiality – What information must not be made known or given to third parties?
- Copyrights – Who owns the tangible components?
- Force majeure – An act of God such as fire or freak electrical storm.
- Incentives – What benefits can the seller receive for aligning with the buyers objectives of time, cost, quality, risk, performance?
- Indemnification – Who is liable for such things as personal injury, damage, accidents?
- Independent contractor – States that the seller is not an employee of the buyer.
- Inspection – Does anyone have a right to inspect the work during execution of the project and under what circumstances?
- Intellectual property – Who owns the intangibles?
- Invoicing –What attachments or supporting documents are required? To whom are they sent and when?
- Liquidated damages – Estimated damages for specific breaches, described in advance.
- Management requirements
- Material breach – A breach so large that it may not be possible to complete the work under the contract.
- Notice – To whom should certain correspondence be sent?
- Patents – Who will own any patents or rules governing the use of existing patents?
- Payments - When will they be made, late payment fees, reasons for non payment?
- Reporting – What reports are required, at what frequency, from and to whom?
- Retainage – An amount of money, usually 5% or 10% withheld from each payment. This money is paid when all the final work is completed and helps ensure completion.
- Scope of work – If not listed separately.
- Site access – Any requirements for access to the site where the work will be performed.
- Termination – Stopping the work before it is completed.
- Time is of the essence – Delivery is strictly binding. Seller is on notice that time is very important and that any delay is a material breach.
- Waiver – Intentionally or unintentionally giving up a right in the contract due to lack of oversight. If you don't require that the Scope of Work or other legal requirements be fulfilled, you could waive your right to get them.

© May 2000 (Registered) Rita Mulcahy, PMP at RMC – Project Management
PHONE: (612) 929-7539, EMAIL: rita@rmcproject.com, WEB: rmcproject.com

STANDARD CONTRACT (OR BOILERPLATE page 131): Companies frequently have standard contracts that are preprinted. If signed, as is, these are legally sufficient and will form a contract.

SPECIAL PROVISIONS: The project manager should consider adding to or changing the standard contract so that it addresses the particular needs of the project. These are sometimes called special provisions and are a result of:
- Risk analysis
- The requirements of the project
- The type of project
- Legal requirements
- Administrative or business requirements

OTHER CONTRACT CONCEPTS:

PRIVITY: Means a contractual relationship. You should understand the following because it explains privity and shows you how questions on this topic are asked.

Company A hires company B to do some work for them. Company B subcontracts to company C. The project manager for A is at the job site and notices there is something wrong with what company C is doing. They say "stop work." Does company C have to listen?

The answer is no; they have no contractual relationship.

LETTER OF INTENT: You should know that this is NOT a contract but simply a letter, without legal binding, that says the buyer intends to hire the seller.

NON-COMPETITIVE FORMS OF PROCUREMENT: Sometimes work is awarded to a company without competition. These are used when:
- The project is under extreme schedule pressure,
- A contractor has unique qualifications,
- There is only one contractor, or
- Other mechanisms exist to ensure that contractor prices are reasonable.

You should be familiar with the following forms:
- SINGLE SOURCE – Contract directly with your preferred seller.
- SOLE SOURCE – There is only one supplier (e.g., they have a patent).

Exercise:

<u>INSTRUCTIONS</u>: Test yourself! What are the unique management challenges for the buyer in managing sole source or single source contracts?

Answer:

Seller could go out of business and seller has no incentive to:

Charge the lowest price
Complete the project on time
Provide good quality
Bankruptcy

EVALUATION CRITERIA (page 128): Are used to rate or score proposals. Evaluation criteria are included in the procurement documents in order to give the seller an understanding of the buyer's needs. When the proposals are received, criteria are used to evaluate and make a selection between sellers. Such criteria may include:

- Understanding of need
- Overall or life cycle cost
- Technical ability
- Management approach
- Financial capacity
- Project management ability (I had to put this in! How many of you require your suppliers or vendors to use the project management techniques you have learned? How about asking for a WBS and Network Diagram?)

~ Evaluation criteria are not commonly used in an IFB situation because the evaluation criteria are simply lowest bidder or lowest responsible bidder.

STEP 3: SOLICITATION (page 129 – 130): The buzzword for this step is "Questions and Answers (Q&A)" and consists of answering seller's questions and receiving proposals or bids.

BIDDER'S CONFERENCE (Proposer's Conference or Pre-Bid Conference, page 129): Used in conjunction with any type of procurement, the bidder's conference is a meeting with prospective sellers to make sure that they all have a clear and common understanding of the procurement. Sellers have a chance to ask questions.

A bidder's conference can be THE key to making sure the pricing in the seller's response matches the work that needs to be done and is therefore the lowest price. Bidder conferences benefit both the buyer and seller. Many project managers do not attend these meetings or realize their importance. The exam often asks what things the project manager must watch out for in a bidder's conference:

- Collusion
- Sellers not asking their questions in front of their competition
- Making sure all questions and answers are put in writing and issued to all potential sellers by the buyer as an addendum to the procurement documents. This insures that all sellers are responding to the same scope of work

QUALIFIED SELLER LISTS (or pre-qualified seller lists, page 129): The seller's qualifications have been checked in advance and the company's name is put on an approved or pre-qualified list. The procurement documents would than be sent only to the pre-qualified sellers.

ADVERTISING (page 129): In order to attract additional sellers, an advertisement may be placed in newspapers, magazines and other places. NOTE: The US government is required to advertise most of its procurements.

STEP 4: SOURCE SELECTION (page 130 - 131): The Buzzword for this step is "PICK ONE" and consists of reviewing the proposals and selecting a seller. In some instances, a seller is "short listed" or put on the list of sellers who will be interviewed. A seller is selected, or short-listed, based on one or a combination of the following:

- Weighting system – Weighting the sellers according to each of the proposal criteria.
- Screening system – Eliminating sellers that do not meet some minimum standard.
- Independent estimate – Comparing the cost to an estimate created in-house or with outside assistance.
- Past performance history – Looking at the seller's past history with the buyer.

NEGOTIATION (page 130): The exam sometimes asks about negotiation and different negotiation tactics. These may amount to only one or two questions.

OBJECTIVES OF NEGOTIATION – Two objectives of negotiation are to:

1. Obtain a fair and reasonable price.
2. Develop a good relationship with the seller.

Most people are surprised by the second item. If you press too strongly during negotiations and the negotiations turn from a win-win (preferable) situation to a win-lose situation, then the seller *will get you back* sometime during the project. In this situation, the project manager will have to spend more time making sure that the seller does not add extra costs, propose unnecessary work or initiate other activities to "win" back what they lost during negotiation. The project manager must be involved during negotiation if for no other reason than to protect the relationship. Many projects go bad because of how negotiations were handled.

NEGOTIATION TACTICS – This is another topic not covered in the PMBOK® but it is sometimes asked on the exam. You should be familiar with the types of negotiation tactics. Here are the simple explanations for each tactic.

TACTICS
EXAMPLE FOR ATTACKS: "If you don't know the details of your own company, perhaps you should get out of the business!"
PERSONAL INSULTS – "If you do not understand what you are doing, perhaps you should find another job!"
GOOD GUY/BAD GUY – One person is helpful to the other side while another is difficult to deal with.
DEADLINE – "We have a flight leaving at 5 PM today and must finish negotiations before that time."
LYING – Not telling the truth. This may be obvious or hidden.
LIMITED AUTHORITY – "I can't agree to shorten the schedule by six months. I have only been authorized to offer three months." Limited authority statements may or may not be true.
MISSING MAN – "Only my boss can agree to that request, and he isn't here. Why don't we agree to only do ____? I can agree to that."
FAIR AND REASONABLE – "Let's be fair and reasonable. Accept this offer as it stands."
DELAY – "Let us revisit this issue the next time we get together." This may also take the form of never actually getting down to negotiating until the last day of a planned visit.
EXTREME DEMANDS – "We planned on giving you the year 2000 compliant software in June 2000."
WITHDRAWAL – This can either be an emotional withdrawal or a physical withdrawal and can show a lessening of interest.
FAIT ACCOMPLI – A done deal. "These government terms and conditions must be in all our contracts."

MAIN ITEMS TO NEGOTIATE (page 130): PMI® says that the main items to negotiate are:

- Responsibilities
- Authority
- Applicable law – Under which law (US state, county, or international) will the contract fall
- Technical and business management approaches
- Contract financing
- Price

Remember that price may not be the primary selection criteria or the primary item to negotiate. Also note that this list may differ from the "real" world.

STEP 5: CONTRACT ADMINISTRATION (page 131 – 132): The buzzword for this step is "ADMIN" and consists of assuring that the seller's performance meets contractual requirements. Project managers have a tendency to ignore the terms and conditions of a contract and focus on what the project manager knows best, the Scope of Work. *This is not acceptable project management.* The project manager must read and understand the contract and manage its completion. The terms and conditions of a contract include work that needs to be done!

CONFLICT: In most projects where a contract is used, another person controls the contract. This person may be called the contracting officer or contract administrator and, in many cases, IS THE ONLY ONE WITH AUTHORITY TO CHANGE THE CONTRACT. We have already said that the contract includes the Scope of Work. You can see the potential for conflict between the contracting officer and the project manager. This type of conflict is frequently a subject of exam questions.

CONTRACT CHANGE CONTROL SYSTEM (page 132): A process for modifying the contract. It is important to note when a contract exists on a project, the project manager's success depends not on his or her teammates but on the culture and procedures of an entirely different company! Sometimes exam questions ask how project control is different in a contracted environment. The answer may include:

- You need to deal with a different company's set of procedures.
- It is not as easy to "see" problems.
- A greater reliance on reports to determine if a problem exists.
- A greater reliance on relationships between the buyer and seller's project managers.

STEP 6: **CONTRACT CLOSE-OUT** (page 133 – 134): The buzzword for this step is "FINISH" and consists of finishing all the loose ends of the contract. Questions on this topic will be easier if you think of contract closeout as containing similar work to project close-out but with more attention to documentation and completion of files. You should be familiar with this part of the PMBOK® and be prepared for up to six questions that ask about this topic, inputs and outputs, as well as how this topic is similar and different than administrative closure in Communications (page 109).

> **LESSONS LEARNED** (OR POST-CONTRACT EVALUATIONS) – Mean the same thing as a project Lessons Learned. In this case they serve as the historical basis for future contractor selection.

> DOCUMENT THE FILE – At the end of a contract a concerted effort must be made to put all files, letters, correspondence, other records of the project, and the contract into an organized file. This helps protect the project in case of arguments or legal action regarding what was done and not done on the project.

OTHER CONTRACT ISSUES ON THE EXAM:

CENTRALIZED, DECENTRALIZED CONTRACTING: Centralized contracting means a separate contracting office handles contracts for all projects. Decentralized contracting means a contract administrator (contracting officer) is assigned to each project.

The exam sometimes asks the advantages and disadvantages of different forms of organizing for managing contracts. To answer any questions like these, simply think of the advantages and disadvantages of centralized project management versus the advantages and disadvantages of centralized contracting.

Exercise:

INSTRUCTIONS: Complete the following chart:

Centralized Contracting	Decentralized Contracting
Advantages	**Advantages**
Disadvantages	**Disadvantages**

Answer:

Centralized Contracting	Decentralized Contracting
Advantages	**Advantages**
Increase expertise in contracting	Easier access to contracting expertise
Standardized company practices	More loyalty to the project
A clearly defined career path for contracting staff	

Disadvantages	Disadvantages
May be difficult to gain access to contracting expertise	No home for the contracts person after the project is completed
One contracts person may work on many projects	Difficult to maintain a high level of contracting expertise in the company
	Duplication of expertise and inefficient use of resources
	Little standardization of contracting practices from one project to the next

CONTRACT INTERPRETATION: In the real world, project managers are always faced with the need to interpret the contract to answer many questions such as: What does the contract really say? Who is responsible for what scope of work?

Contract interpretation is never easy and frequently requires the assistance of a lawyer. However, the exam may describe a simple situation about a conflict over interpretation of a contract and ask you to interpret the correct answer. Contract interpretation is based on an analysis of the intent of the parties to the contract and a few guidelines. One such guideline is that the contract supercedes any memos, conversations or discussions that may have occurred prior to the contract signing. Therefore, if a requirement is not in the contract, even if it was agreed upon, it does not have to be met.

The following is an exercise on intent. The correct answers more clearly show the intent of the parties to the contract.

Exercise: Contract Interpretation Exercise – "WHICH WINS"

<u>INSTRUCTIONS</u>: On each line, circle the item that would "win" in a dispute over contract interpretation.

Contract language	OR	A memo describing changes after the contract is signed
Contract language	OR	A memo signed by both parties before the contract is signed that describes what was agreed to during negotiations
Contract terms and conditions	OR	Scope of work
Common definition	OR	The intended meaning (without supplying a definition)
Industry use of the term	OR	Common use of term
Special provisions	OR	General provisions
Typed over wording on the contract	OR	A handwritten comment on the contract that is also initialed
Numbers	OR	Words
Detailed terms	OR	General terms

Answer: Contract Interpretation Exercise – "WHICH WINS"

<u>Contract language</u>	OR	A memo describing changes after the contract is signed
<u>Contract language</u>	OR	A memo signed by both parties before the contract is signed that describes what was agreed to during negotiations
Contract terms and conditions	OR	Scope of work
It depends! This is decided in the Order of Precedence Clause in the contract.		
<u>Common definition</u>	OR	The intended meaning (without supplying a definition)
<u>Industry use of the term</u>	OR	Common use of term
<u>Special provisions</u>	OR	General provisions
Typed over wording on the contract	OR	**<u>A handwritten comment on the contract that is also initialed</u>**
Numbers	OR	**<u>Words</u>**
<u>Detailed terms</u>	OR	General terms

SAMPLE QUESTIONS
Procurement Management

	3rd Time	2nd Time	1st Time

1) Once signed a contract is legally binding unless:
   A. One party is unwilling to perform
   B. One party is unable to finance his part of the work
   C. It is in violation of applicable law
   D. It is declared null and void by one party

2) With a clear Scope of Work a contractor completes work as specified, but the buyer is not pleased with the results. The contract is considered to be:
   A. Incomplete because the buyer is not pleased
   B. Incomplete because the specs are incorrect
   C. Complete because the contractor is satisfied
   D. Complete because the contractor met the terms and conditions (T & C's) of the contract

3) Which of the following statements concerning bid documentation is/are correct?
   A. Well-designed bid documentation can simplify comparison of responses
   B. Bid documentation must be rigorous with no flexibility to allow consideration of seller suggestions
   C. Bid documents should generally not include evaluation criteria
   D. A and C

4) Although they may have a variety of side effects, the primary objective of incentive clauses in a contract is to:
   A. Reduce costs for the buyer
   B. Help the contractor control costs
   C. Help bring the contractor's objectives in line with that of the buyer
   D. Reduce risk for the contractor by shifting risk to the buyer

5) Which statement regarding change control is correct?
   A. A FP contract will minimize the need for change control
   B. Changes seldom provide real benefits to the project
   C. Contracts should include procedures to accommodate changes
   D. More detailed specifications will eliminate the most common causes of changes

6) A routine audit of a cost reimbursable contract determines that overcharges are being made to the contract. If the contract does not specify corrective action, the buyer should:

    A.   Continue to make payments
    B.   Halt payments until the problem is corrected
    C.   Void the contract and start legal action to recover overpayments
    D.   Change the contract to require more frequent audits

7) The primary objective of negotiations is to:

    A.   Get the most from the other side
    B.   Protect the relationship
    C.   Be the winner
    D.   Define your objectives up front and stick with them

8) A seller is working on a cost reimbursable contract when the buyer decides he would like to expand the scope of services and change to a fixed price contract. The seller's options include:

    A.   Completing the original work on a cost reimbursable basis and then negotiating a fixed price for the additional work
    B.   Completing the original work and rejecting the additional work
    C.   Negotiating a fixed price contract that includes all the work
    D.   All of the above

9) Bidder's conferences are part of:

    A.   Solicitation planning
    B.   Contract administration
    C.   Solicitation
    D.   Procurement planning

10) Which of the following must be present to have a contract?

    A.   A detailed scope of work
    B.   Acceptance
    C.   The address of the seller
    D.   Some legal words

11) Which of the following best describes the project manager's role during the contracting process?

    A.   They are not involved
    B.   They should try to be involved
    C.   They supply an understanding of the risks of the project
    D.   They tell the contracts manager how they want the contracting process to be handled

12) A key role of the project manager during negotiations is to:

    A.   Protect the relationship between buyer and seller
    B.   Make sure their side wins
    C.   Make sure they get all the risks assigned to the other side
    D.   Make sure they receive a communication plan

13) Procurement planning involves:
 A. A make or buy decision
 B. Answering seller's questions
 C. Creating the contract
 D. Creating the RFP

14) Which of the following is not part of contract administration?
 A. Evaluating risks
 B. Confirming submittals have been sent
 C. Confirming that changes to the contract are made
 D. Answering questions of potential sellers

15) In a cost plus fixed fee contract, the fee:
 A. Never changes
 B. Changes if change orders are issued
 C. Is small
 D. Will always decrease

16) In a fixed price contract, the fee or profit is:
 A. Unknown
 B. Part of the negotiation involved in paying every invoice
 C. Applied as a line item to every invoice
 D. Determined with the other party at the end of the project

17) A disadvantage of a cost reimbursable contract for the seller is that the buyer needs to:
 A. Pay more per month
 B. Audit seller's costs
 C. Constantly evaluate the fee it is paying
 D. Write a detailed scope of work

18) An advantage of a fixed price contract for the buyer is:
 A. The seller has the cost risk
 B. The buyer has the cost risk
 C. There is little risk
 D. The risk is very high

19) Which of the following is not part of the contract documents?
 A. The proposal
 B. The scope of work
 C. The terms and conditions
 D. Negotiation notes

20) Stating that you only have one hour to make your plane is an example of what type of negotiation technique?
 A. Good guy, bad guy
 B. Delay
 C. Deadline
 D. Extreme demands

21) Which of the following is an advantage of centralized contracting?
 A. Easier access to contracting expertise
 B. Increased company expertise in contracting
 C. More loyalty to the project
 D. No home for the contracts personnel

22) The seller is most concerned about project scope in a _____ type of contract?
 A. Fixed price
 B. Cost plus fixed fee
 C. Time and Material
 D. Cost plus primary fee

23) Your company has an emergency and needs some work done as soon as possible. Which of the following would be the most helpful to add to the contract under these circumstances?
 A. A clear scope of work
 B. Requirements as to which subcontractors can be used
 C. Incentives
 D. A force majeure clause

24) Contract negotiation occurs during which step of the procurement process?
 A. Procurement Planning
 B. Solicitation Planning
 C. Solicitation
 D. Source Selection

25) Proposals are received during which step of the procurement process?
 A. Procurement Planning
 B. Solicitation Planning
 C. Solicitation
 D. Source Selection

26) A decision to make or buy is made during which step of the procurement process?
 A. Procurement planning
 B. Solicitation Planning
 C. Solicitation
 D. Source Selection

27) An RFP is issued during which step of the procurement process?
 A. Procurement Planning
 B. Solicitation Planning
 C. Solicitation
 D. Source Selection

28) A contractor has withdrawn from your project. A new contractor has been established. His labor forces are due to arrive at the job site tomorrow. You should?

    A.   Meet with the contractor and his forces and establish yourself as the authority in charge

    B.   Bring your team in for introductions and establish a communications exchange

    C.   Bring out the communications plan

    D.   Bring out the project plan

ANSWERS

1 C
2 D
3 A
4 C
5 C
6 A
7 B
8 D
9 C
10 B
11 C
12 A
13 A
14 D
15 B
16 A
17 B
18 A
19 D
20 C
21 B
22 A
23 C
24 D
25 C
26 A
27 B
28 A

Bibliography

Most experienced and trained project managers who use these materials and the PMBOK® to study do not need other materials to pass the exam. However, if you are not so experienced or have never had training in project management by someone who was a PMP® and there are some topics in these materials that you would like to learn more about, let me recommend the following additional reading.

Basic reading for everyone: One of PMI®'s main sources for questions is a series of pamphlets on project management now published as the following book.
- ***Principles of Project Management*** by the Project Management Institute, ISBN: 1-880410-30-3.
  This book has chapters on:
    - Conflict management
    - Contracts
    - Negotiation
    - Forms of organization for project management
    - Roles and responsibilities
    - Team building

Another source of sample questions:
- ***PMBOK Q&A*** by the Project Management Institute, ISBN: 1-880410-21-4

Basic project management textbook often used at universities:
- ***Project Management: A Managerial Approach*** by authors Meredith and Mantel , ISBN: 0-471-01626-8

A real world book on project management that is becoming very highly regarded. This book has some great coverage of scheduling and PERT.
- ***Project Planning, Scheduling and Control*** by James Lewis, ISBN: 1-55738-869-5

A great summary of project management for experienced project managers:
- ***Fast Forward MBA in Project Management*** by Eric Verzuh, ISBN: ISBN:0-471-32546-5

Index